LET LOVE LEAD

BILL BENNOT

LET LOVE LEAD
First edition 2018
ISBN 978-0-620-76194-9

© 2018 Bill Bennot

Published by:

FAITH Story
P U B L I S H I N G

Making God Famous by Telling His story

Faith Story Publishing
1 Tarentaal Avenue Mooivalleipark, Potchefstroom, 2531
PO Box 20288, Noordbrug, 2522

Requests for information should be addressed to:
Faith Story Publishing
PO Box 20288, Noordbrug, 2522

My friend, Bill Bennot, is a passionate, loving, pioneer & warrior. He's lived a life of faithfully walking toward Jesus who has the sword of truth pointed at his heart. This sword penetrating his life is what is in these pages. In quick chapters, Bill shows you his lessons and gains in learning to 'Let Love Lead'. I always love to learn about someone's victories who I know has truly lived them out. Bill Bennot is a man on a mission and a man changed by that mission. I think you'll be both challenged and changed as you read Let Love Lead.

Danny Silk *(Author of many best sellers, including Culture and Honor, Keep Your Love On and Powerful and Free)*

I love reading books by authors who are authentic to their message. Bill Bennot, in his book, Let Love Lead writes from a life well lived in the trenches of ministry and relationships; and he has the scars to prove it. Amazingly, those scares have not made him bitter or jaded but have become badges of the apostolic grace that is evident in Bill's calling and life. It is the way he wears his scars that make me proud to call him a friend.

I highly recommend Let Love Lead to every leader that has the courage to lead from the inside out. Bills words will challenge your hearts position as it relates to how you love God, yourself, and the people around you. They will not leave you condemned, just greatly challenged. Read this book with personal transformation in mind, and you will not be disappointed.

David Crone *(Senior Leader of 'The Mission' in Vacaville, California)*

I highly recommend Bill Bennot's book Let Love Lead. Bill releases powerful and practical I Corinthians 13 revelation on the needed topic of love in leadership. The whole book is great, but the table of contents alone will rock your world. Thanks, Bill, for your continual pursuit of healthy living and healthy leadership.

Steve Backlund *(Prolific author and leader of Igniting Hope Ministries)*

Though Bill wrote this book for leaders, I think he is wrong. This is a book for absolutely everyone. Not since The Ragamuffin Gospel, has a publication so impacted me. I've read hundreds of books on the A, B, C's of leadership, and to pigeonhole Let Love Lead, into that category does it a disservice.

Let Love Lead reveals what the Gospel is meant to look like. With eloquence, humor, and story, Bill paints a portrait of a leader with no agenda, nothing to prove, utterly vulnerable, and with everything to give. The trend over the years has been to run churches like businesses. Often it seems as if each church is its own little kingdom with its own little king. Let Love Lead smashes the idea of the church business and reveals the true message of Christ. I can't adequately put into words how vital and revolutionary this book is for this generation.

Joel Clark *(Author, Adventurer and Film Maker)*

Bill's endless enthusiasm and love for people are not simply an abstract that he writes about but what he embodies. You will be tremendously blessed by this book.

Jamie George *(Pastor and author in Nashville Tennessee)*

To my amazing wife, Connie.

You have inspired me and contributed to my leadership journey like no one else could. After 36 years of marriage, I still wake up amazed that God would bless me with such a treasure as you.

ACKNOWLEDGEMENTS

Toni Hutchinson, *thank you for your eagle eye and tireless effort in the editing process. Your heart always amazes me.*

Stacy Black, *thank you for your creative touch and humble service in finding the right design for the cover. You are such a treasure.*

Costa Mitchell, *thank you for pastoring me through my most difficult seasons. Also, a lot of what I have written in this book I have watched in you over the years.*

To my Journey of Grace community and family in Cape Town, *thank you for making room for the experiment of 'Let Love Lead.' In spite of the pressures of the status quo, you have continued to say yes to the new wine and the new wineskin.*

A special thanks to all the leaders and friends *walking with me in BMosaic and beyond. Thank you for being the evidence of 'Let Love Lead.' It takes lots of humility, courage and stamina, as well as a little bit of 'crazy' to motor on for no other reasons than knowing God, loving people, advancing the kingdom and glorifying Jesus.*

TABLE OF CONTENTS

PART I - WHO WE ARE

FOREWORD

E very author, when reading someone else's writing on a subject loved by the reader, has doubtless had several moments when they have slapped their forehead and said: "I wish I had written that!" That very thing happened to me when reading this book. This is a series of "WOW!" moments waiting to happen to you!

I know Bill Bennot well. I have known him, and heard him, and read him, for over thirty years. "Let Love Lead", however, is a staggeringly delightful piece de resistance, a deceptively short but rich opus magnum. It is Bill at his best, using words in brilliant couplets and contrasting rhythms, with deep and profound significance not only in every page, but in almost every line! Bill Bennot is sharing his life's longing in these pages, and I guarantee you will want more when you reach its end.

I kept thinking – this is so good, it needs to be elaborated on. And yet, its genius and impact is in its brevity and punchiness, its humility and understated depth. Like a great meal, its beauty is in the fact that it leaves you wanting more.

I found it not only informative and entrancing, but deeply moving. It is a masterful summation of everything life has taught him, illustrated with great quotes, each one well positioned and apt to the point he is making. He writes as a preacher, and every chapter resonates with the longing of a heart that seeks a better way to do leadership, to lead God's people, with simple authenticity. With integrity. With Love.

Enjoy letting Love Lead you through these pages. Then, step out of the book into a more excellent way.

Costa Mitchell *(Founder and Director of Vineyard, South Africa and part of the global leadership of Vineyard Churches International. Author of 'Intimacy in Marriage' and 'Giving Leadership.')*

INTRODUCTION

The event occurred over 30 years ago, yet I remember it like it was yesterday. I had just bought my second vehicle since moving to South Africa. It was a Mitsubishi Star Wagon. I was quite proud of having made this purchase. It was the first time Connie and I had acquired financing from a South African bank. South Africa was starting to feel more like home. I just had the vehicle serviced, and we were driving home in the evening when it suddenly stopped running. I was able to pull into the parking lot of a business owned by a friend. After making a few phone calls, I located the mechanic who had serviced our vehicle. He promptly came out to where we were stranded. I could sense his anxiety as he began to investigate the problem. He found that the head gasket was blown and the camshaft had seized. In a defensive and fearful tone, he said, "This is not my breakdown." He was preparing to be blamed. His defenses shot up like a rocket. Without a second thought, I responded, "Hey don't worry, it's going to be ok. You are more important than my camshaft." I think both of us were a bit surprised by my response. I found myself being more concerned about him feeling threatened than about being stranded and without a working car.

I am not always so magnanimous under pressure. I have disappointed myself many times for not demonstrating better calm and sensitivity. But in that moment I *let love lead*. I had plenty of reason to respond differently. I was stuck and faced with an expensive repair, which I had no finances for – and he had worked on our vehicle the day before. Yet in that moment I truly cared more about him than my car or the immediate need. It was as if my soul was in alignment with this love that doesn't fail.

From my earliest days after becoming a Christian, I was utterly captured by the love of Jesus. I was totally undone by the fact that Almighty God knew and loved me. I was so amazed by what his love did that my number one prayer became: "Father, help me to love like Jesus loves." I can remember praying that prayer almost every day for years. I believe God answered my prayer by making me very sensitive to people and their needs. I would find myself caring about people very quickly, and often way beyond my ability to do much with it. Honestly, at times I regretted praying that prayer. God would give me His heart for someone, but I would often lack the capacity or resources to respond accordingly. It's like being extremely hungry, but your stomach has no room for food. It's like being with someone you genuinely care about, but they don't know who you are. My desire to give was often frustrated by my personal shortcomings. It seemed to cause me more grief than joy. It set me up for a lot of disappointment. The human soul is not meant to carry disappointment for long periods of time. When disappointment lingers too long in the soul it fosters discouragement, disillusionment and cynicism. Well, I found the remedy in my calling as a servant-leader.

If the truth be told, I stopped praying that prayer every day. Loving like Jesus is still my great passion, but now I focus on specific things that make it a reality. I am more interested in what love looks like as a leader. I see my calling to serve and lead others as the primary vehicle for this 'never failing love.' I am much more intentional about the values, beliefs, behaviors, actions, strategies, and systems that actualize and demonstrate love.

To 'have love' and not 'do love' is a painful proposition. There are only two times recorded in the Gospels where Jesus wept. Once, just before raising Lazarus from the dead, and the other was when he entered Jerusalem for the last time. Both of these moments highlight the pain that comes with having more desire to give to others than can actually be received. As Jesus said, "Oh Jerusalem, Jerusalem how I longed to gather you like a hen gathers her chicks, but you were unwilling." In our relationship with Jesus, any unwillingness to receive or give is always on our side, but in our relationship with others, it goes both ways.

We are creatures made from and for love, and our truest happiness is only found when we live and lead from that design. That being said, what does love look like for a leader and in leading? Jesus did not just teach on love, he lived and labored from love. He demonstrated love more in his walk than in his talk. He did it more than he said it. His entire lifestyle and ministry was a demonstration of love. Consider parents and their children. From the day that little Ben or Melody comes from the womb, every behavior or action towards them comes from love. It's literally love incarnate. Whether midnight feeding, hourly nappy changing or constant cuddling, love is on display. Love leads the entire relationship. No one has to ask, "Are you loving Ben and Melody?" They can see it in almost every action.

This book is not about defining love, and makes no attempt to address the different kinds of love. We already have vast numbers of great books that do that. It's simply about what love looks like in the outfit of a leader. When love wears a leader there are attitudes, motivations, behaviors, actions, and effects that are incorruptible and indestructible. I have had the privilege of traveling a leadership journey for over 37 years. I am still a student of love and leading, but I have come to know, to some degree, what it looks like when love leads. *Let Love Lead* is my gift to all those servant-leaders who desire to love and lead like Jesus.

Of the many attitudes, motivations, behaviors, actions, and effects that love looks like when leading, I have selected only twenty. Quite frankly, since love is eternal because God is love and he is eternal, we can never model love's entire leadership wardrobe. But we can present those outfits that are most impacting and activating. I have organized the twenty outfits in three categories. The first ten address *who we are*, the next five cover *who others are* and the last five focus on *who we are together*. Enjoy.

PART I

WHO
WE ARE

1

You let love lead when you don't care who gets the credit as long as God gets the glory.

There are few things more egregious than a leader who is overly concerned with 'who gets the credit.' Being recognized for our labors is a good thing, but making that our focus is to miss the heart of good leadership, which is growth and productivity. Meaning, if ground is being gained, lives are being improved and Jesus is being glorified, then it shouldn't matter who gets the credit.

Being a good leader starts at the breastbone and not the backbone. Our hearts have more impact on the quality of how we lead than all our heaving lifting. The writer of Proverbs emphasized this point with, "Watch over your heart with all diligence, for from it flows the springs of life" (Proverbs 4:23). We often underestimate the power of our own hearts. What comes out of our hearts, which is the core of our moral being, can either contaminate a good action or redeem a bad choice. In leadership, heart attitudes matter more than gifts, skills or experience. Paul told the Philippians to have the same attitude as Jesus did (Philippians 2:5). He humbled himself as a servant rather than exalting himself as a superior.

I love Paul's attitude on this point. He told the believers in Philippi that some people preach the gospel out of selfish ambition, rather than from pure motives. He said that they wanted to cause him distress while in prison. He finishes the thought with, "Whether pretense or in truth, Christ is proclaimed; and in this I rejoice" (Philippians 1:18) While writing to the Philippians, Paul was in prison, and there were leaders in Philippi who envied his relationship with the church. They were now reaping from his arduous labors. He was content with them being recognized, as long as Jesus was being preached. Because he let love lead, he cared less about who was getting credit and more about Jesus receiving the glory.

There are different reasons for 'credit hunting.' Everything from personal insecurities to organizational styles can make gaining recognition more important than bringing the kingdom of Jesus. There is plenty written about insecurity in the human heart. If we do not get our identity and affirmation from the God who created us, we will pursue it elsewhere. Self-aggrandizement and self-promotion are sad but common behaviors in the leadership industry. An 'all about me' attitude can be found everywhere, but to see it in the Body of Christ is even more grievous. There is another cause for 'credit hogging' that can often go unnoticed. It has to do with how we view our ministries and local churches.

Ever since Constantine and the Edict of Milan in 313 AD, the institution of the Church has, at times, warred against the real identity of the Church. It's where the structures, strategies, systems and styles of our local churches become less compatible to the work of the Holy Spirit in every believer. We are the Body of Christ, but we often live like an assortment of limbs – like a bunch of disconnected body parts. We are the Bride of Christ, and yet sometimes we look more like the Bride of Frankenstein. When God calls us a family, some leaders act as though he means *the Sopranos*. Once you are in, you better not leave – and if you do you are dead. Some local churches act more like competing businesses, measuring success by their share of the 'people market.' They use language like, 'our people' and get very upset when any of 'their people' drift to a neighboring congregation. As long as church leaders privatize membership (our people), monopolize discipleship (our way), bureaucratize fellowship (our structure) and centralize leadership (our authority), the Church will function as an assortment of limbs in buildings, rather than as the Body of Christ in cities. When an organization ceases to serve its God-given purpose, it tends toward bureaucracy, morphs into institutionalism and becomes the purpose.

Now most pastors and church leaders would abhor this kind of mentality or effect, but some of our ministry approaches and practices have created this problem. One of the best preventions against the privatizing of local churches comes from having an apostolic or kingdom perspective. Meaning, rather than looking at the community through the lens of our local church, we must look at our local church through the lens of what God is doing in the broader community. To the degree that we will build as the Body of Christ in our city is the degree to which God's kingdom will have more impact in our city. I will say more about the apostolic later. Following is a proclamation of identity that comes from an apostolic leadership perspective. It highlights the priority of Holy Spirit power shaping kingdom-oriented form.

We, the Church, are not the buildings we own, the programs we join, the services we attend, the membership databases we fill, the leadership positions we support, the ministry events we create or the corporate branding we share.

We are merely people who follow Jesus everywhere and do authentic life with others. We hear God's voice, and we take responsibility for what that looks like in our life journeys. Any structures, strategies, systems or tools we employ have one primary objective: more of God's goodness anywhere. We believe the Bible, and we love its author.

We are organized, but we aren't an organization. We have a corporate culture, but we aren't a corporation. We have leaders in our lives, but leaders don't own our lives. We are busy bringing God's kingdom, but we build no human fiefdoms. We are part of a local community, but not confined to one community. We are definitely accountable to people but defined by no one but God.

We would rather serve than be served, and giving is our favorite pastime. We build upon the past, but never camp around it. We have our hearts in heaven, but our hands on the plow. We celebrate our diversity and embrace our unity. We encourage everyone, and we police no one.

We are called to know God and love people, and what that looks like is everyone's choice and personal responsibility. We will go the extra mile with anyone, but we are a doormat for no one. We know we have weaknesses, but they never rule over us. We are crazy about Jesus, and we don't care who knows it. We are the Church, and Jesus gets all the glory.

2

You let love lead when you easily and gladly do the unnoticed things.

C ontinuing with my previous statement about good leadership starting at the breastbone rather than the backbone – it's what we are and do that others don't see that determines the character and quality of what they do see. Real leadership begins below the skin and behind the scenes. It's motivated from their nature before driving them towards their future. It's who they are before it's what they do. For a good leader, serving is its own reward. This is the domain of servant- leadership. There is a difference between leaders who serve and real servant-leaders. The former will use people to serve a plan, while the latter will use a plan to serve people.

D.L. Moody said that the real measure of a man is not in how many servants he has, but by how many men he serves.

That thought is modeled best by the life and ministry of Jesus. Jesus told us that he "did not come to be served, but to serve" (Matthew 20:25). Everything Jesus did, from taking away the sins of the world to healing all who were oppressed by the devil, came from the heart of a servant. Servant-leadership is by no means a new concept. Our first picture of the Creator in Genesis Chapter's 1 and 2 presents a God who serves, who labors for the benefit of others. The writer of Hebrews points out that Jesus is the exact representation of God's nature. Our first impression of God isn't some bossy dictator saying, 'Gabriel do this and Michael do that!' The phrases we find are, "God created," "God made," "God blessed," "God gave," "God formed," "God planted" and "God built." This is the nature of the Holy Spirit. Jesus said, "The Father will send you another helper" (one who comes alongside to help). In God's economy, leadership and servanthood are two sides of the same coin.

In Herman Hess's book, *Journey to the East*, we find a great example of how the servant comes before the leader. In the story, there is a group of men on a journey. They are accompanied by Leo who is the essential character in the story. Leo was the servant to these men. He does all the chores as well as strengthens them with his spirit and song. Then one day Leo disappears. The journey is abandoned as the group begins to fall apart. The obvious point is that they cannot make it without Leo. After many years of wandering, one of the men finds Leo and brings him into the Order that had sponsored the journey. To his surprise, he discovers that Leo is the great and noble leader of the Order. What stands out from this narrative is that Leo was the leader all the time, but what mattered most was that he was first and foremost a servant. Leading them effectively meant serving them daily. It was this story that provided Robert Greenleaf with inspiration for his seminal work on servant-leadership. According to Mr. Greenleaf, "The servant leader is servant first. It begins with the natural feeling that one wants to serve, to serve first. Then conscious choice brings one to aspire to lead. That person is sharply different from one who is leader first, perhaps because of a need to assuage an unusual power drive or to acquire material possessions. For such, it will be a later choice to serve after leadership is established. The leader first and the servant first are two extreme types."

A good illustration of how God prioritizes the servant-leader is found in the Book of Joshua. God is speaking to Joshua about the end of Moses' leadership and the beginning of his own. His last words to Joshua about Moses is quite telling. Usually the last words, the epithet, are a summary of a person's best qualities and greatest achievements. Joshua was about to take over the senior leadership role, and God wanted him to understand what mattered most. Instead of 'Moses the miracle worker,' or 'Moses the great leader,' it was "Moses My servant." In just a handful of verses, God used the word *servant* five times to describe Moses. When the Lord first begins to speak to Joshua, the narrative starts with, "The Lord spoke to Joshua, Moses' servant." In other words, "Joshua I am not asking you to be something brand new, just be more of what you already are, a servant." If it was good enough for Moses and Joshua, then it's good enough for any of God's leaders.

It is one thing for God to understand this fundamental

requirement for leadership, but it's quite another for leaders to. In 2 Samuel 7, we find David referring to himself as a servant eight times in eleven verses. One of the founding fathers of America, George Washington, signed all of his letters with, "Your most humble and obedient servant." Paul called himself a "Bondservant of Christ." The fact that he described himself in this manner to the church in Rome is very significant. There were more slaves in Rome than free people. Rome was a thriving metropolis because of all its servants. Dictators don't build cities, servants do. In other words, if we are going to build successfully then we must build as servants. Robert Greenleaf's thesis captures this notion. He wrote, "This is my thesis: caring for persons, the more able and the less able serving each other, is the rock upon which a good society is built." Paul went on to tell the believers in Corinth, "I have made myself a servant of all that I might win some" (1 Corinthians 9:19). This is true in context and in principle. If we want to win in the workplace, then we must serve more. If we're going to win in our marriages and families, then we must be servants to them.

Servant leadership emphasizes the leader's role as a steward of the resources (human, financial and otherwise) provided by the organization. It encourages the leader to serve others while staying focused on achieving results that are in line with shared values and vision. The servant-leader abstains from the more common top-down hierarchical approach and embraces collaboration, trust, empathy, and the ethical use of power. A pastor modeling servant leadership will identify congregational needs prior to strategy and labor. This is in contrast to the leader who labors according to a predetermined agenda, (i.e., their personal mission and goals). Any political leader espousing servant leadership will run for office to serve the needs of their community, not to further career ambitions and agendas. The high school rugby coach acting as a servant first seeks the development of his players before the attainment of fame. In their book, *Lead like Jesus*, Blanchard and Hodges measure the degree of servant leadership by asking the following question, "How well am I doing in preparing others to take my place when the time comes?" The 'servant first' approach helps to guarantee a leadership culture where personal responsibility is premium. It creates a culture where 'everyone a leader' can germinate and spread like wildfire throughout the local church, community and city.

Not everyone can solve complex problems, manage large corporations, develop culture shifting strategies, create market altering tools and technologies, lead history – making teams or inspire next generation leaders, but everyone can serve – everyone can prioritize the needs of others and make a difference. Start where you are. Whether at home, at work or in your community, practice helping others where the act of serving is the reward. Few things reward the soul like the priority of others, and there is nothing that lets love lead quite like a 'servant-first' heart.

3

You let love lead when you can see more or better than there is.

In his book, *The One Thing You Need to Know,* Marcus Buckingham makes a case for his one "satisfactory" definition of a leader. He said, "From all my research, this is the only satisfactory definition I've found: Great leaders rally people to a better future... He is a leader, if and only if, he can rally others to the *better future he sees.*" Although some might not agree with such a narrow description for a leader, few would disagree that the role of vision casting and buy-in are critical to leading successfully. We can't go where we cannot see. That being said, our ability to see bigger and better starts with the heart (our nature) before it focuses on the horizons (what's there). Once again, it's a product of who we are below the skin.

Each person is designed by God to see. Someone's

'vision' is simply their ability to see what's ahead of them. People telling you what something looks like will never be as empowering or as satisfying as you seeing it for yourself. How many people enjoy driving behind a large semi-tractor trailer truck? Probably no one. I have asked that question of hundreds of people, and I've yet to find someone who prefers it. The primary reason we don't like it is that we can't see what's down the road. The backend of that truck is blocking a bigger and better view. Well, what if you had a friend in a car that was ahead of the truck, and they had you on your cell phone and were describing to you what they were seeing? Would you enjoy driving behind that truck any better? Probably not. Why? Because we are all created by God to see for ourselves. This is where we find the reciprocating relationship between vision and values.

There are many kinds of values, but the most basic values, which are the primary motivators in our lives, are actual expressions of our fundamental design or nature. It's who we are. The reason we value food and water is because we are designed to need it. It's not just what we want, it's what we are. We literally can't exist without it. Going back to the relationship between vision and values, the act of seeing and the essence of being are inseparable. Our physical eyesight mirrors this point.

The most basic reason why someone can see the beauty of the Grand Canyon is that their eyes are designed for sight. Being able to see the Grand Canyon is not just by virtue of the canyon's existence. No matter how clearly a tour guide describes the landscape of the Grand Canyon, it will not improve a blind person's ability to see it or hike in it. Some visionary leaders assume that people will see a vision simply because they preach it or teach it ad-nauseam. Without corresponding values in the heart of the people, a vision is little more than cheerleading. A newly married couple may have a vision for a beautiful life together, but without values such as honesty, humility and servanthood it's little more than a fantasy. Connie and I have counseled couples that we could see no positive future for – simply because they lacked the heart standards necessary for obtaining that future.

The fact that seeing better and bigger begins in the heart refutes the notion that it's by virtue of our talents, opportunities or experiences. It's true that specific opportunities make it easier, and enjoyable experiences in life have a way of reinforcing a positive outlook, but every individual is given a measure of faith, or the ability to believe and see more than there is. Our heart's ability to believe or trust is the real driver for living bigger and better. A heart that is riddled with fear and unbelief will see very little regardless of how fortunate the current landscape is. Even a person's gifting or calling is no guarantee that they will see better and bigger. I have worked with very gifted leaders, who have walked in their calling for dozens of years, but through significant disappointment or hurts they abandoned their child-like faith. In spite of their abilities and experience, they see little and doubt everything. Their child-like faith got sidelined by fear and unbelief. One of the best discoveries I ever made in my relationship with Jesus is that God hides a lot in a little, and it's this childlike faith that keeps me discovering more.

In 1 Kings 18, we find one of the most transformational moments in the history of Israel. In one brief moment a nation-wide oppression was removed, all the false prophets were destroyed and three-and-a-half years of drought ended. Elijah, God's prophet, had challenged the prophets of Baal to a 'Who is God' contest, and God won. After the dispensing of the false prophets in the Kishon River, Elijah went back to the top of Mount Carmel. It says that he got into a crouched position, with his face between his knees. This is an intercessory position. His face was between two places. He is brokering the partnership between heaven and earth.

While in this position he tells his servant to go and look toward the sea for a coming storm. It's important to understand what his servant was expecting to see. In verse 41 the servant hears Elijah say, "I hear the sound of the roar of a mighty rain." Meaning, he is expecting to see a big storm. He comes back the first time and says that he sees nothing. Elijah sends him back for another look. Once again he returns without seeing the storm. The servant is sent back seven times. On his seventh return, he tells Elijah, "I see a cloud the size of a man's hand." That tiny cloud he sees was enough for Elijah to send him to the King with the news of an advancing rain storm. I believe that small cloud was there before his seventh look. Drought does not mean a cloudless sky. That cloud may have been there on his first trip. Elijah was not just praying for the mighty rain, he was praying for his servant to see it in that little cloud. Paul told the Roman believers that what was written in earlier times was written for our instruction (Romans 15:4). Meaning, this is not about Elijah and his servant – it's about Jesus and us. Jesus is interceding for us to see a lot in a little, the more in a few. God is the expert at packing more in less. All of us have had experiences where God put a lot in small places, tight spaces and even behind some unlikely faces. How about Moses' staff in delivering Israel, or David's one stone defeating Goliath, or the five loaves and two fish feeding five thousand? Has anyone noticed that God will often ask us to do what is very difficult, and with not enough to do it? Why? To help protect us from the deception that we can ever do great things without God. Consider this: if we always had a surplus when attempting new things, we would start living from the certainty of 'more' rather than the certainty of Him. This is not to suggest that having more isn't important, but when love leads it sees and acts bigger and better before it's bigger and better.

We can all experience drought or lack at certain times in our lives. But in every drought, there is a cloud the size of a man's hand. Jesus is interceding for us to see it. The Holy Spirit wants to show you your mighty rain. Take a moment and see an area of your life that is characterized by lack or loss. Now invite Jesus into that situation. Ask the Holy Spirit to show you your cloud the size of a man's hand. One of two things will happen: you will either see something you have never seen before, or something you have always seen will suddenly take on a redemptive quality. You will soon find faith filling your heart for that situation. Then, just as Elijah told his servant to go to the King with a message, the Holy Spirit will give you some action of faith to take. When obedience follows faith, heaven shows up in force.

4

You let love lead when you are turning hope into an experience.

Hope, like a revelation or a promise, is not the goal or the destination. It's an entry point; an invitation to more; the beautiful possibilities. This should seem obvious, but unfortunately there are millions of believers trying to live off the 'idea' of what could be or should be. They are happily camped out around the promise of fire, with no fire. They are like customers at a restaurant who seem content to just read the menu, pay for a meal they never received and then leave. Hope is a powerful and beautiful thing, but it serves another purpose, experience. I heard Bill Johnson once say that someone with an experience is much more powerful than someone with an argument. Equally true, someone with experience is the best argument. There is nothing that represents the glory of Christianity like people who experience what Jesus paid for.

Once again I refer to the efficacy of our nature or design. The reason we can experience love for and with another person is because our nature requires it, and our design generates it. Our body and soul is wired for the experience of love. In like manner, our nature as children of God requires an experience with God. We have been made to encounter God; spirit, soul and body. The reason I press in for more encounters with God is because my relationship with him and his word requires it. Of course, God's word (the Bible) takes precedence over any personal experience, but God's word is given as a catalyst for personal experience. What God says is the precursor to what God does. From, "He sent His word and healed them," to "I am watching over my word to perform it," to "Our gospel did not come to you in word only, but also in power...," to "The word of God is living and active...," the scripture reminds us over and over again that experience is the purpose of his word (Psalms 107:20, Jeremiah 1:12, 1 Thessalonians 1:5, Hebrews 4:12). Bill Johnson also said that any revelation that does not lead to more encounters with God tends to make us more religious. Church history is proof of that sad reality. As believers, our life must be more than good rhetoric. It must be heavenly reality becoming earthly actuality. No one modeled this better than Jesus.

We find an interesting dialogue between Jesus and a lawyer. The lawyer asks, "What shall I do to inherit eternal life" (Luke 10:25)? The lawyer was putting Jesus to the test. This is a rhetorical question. He was looking for a response that agreed with his position. Jesus responds, "What does the word say, how does it read to you?" Then without any hesitation, the lawyer recites the word. This lawyer knows the word. Lawyers were experts in the Mosaic Law. He was in the word business. Initially, the lawyer's tone seems clear and confident, but suddenly his tone changes. In response to Jesus' next comment the scripture reads, "But wishing to justify himself, he said to Jesus, "And who is my neighbor?"" He goes from clear and confident to uncertain and defensive. Why? Because Jesus added something to the equation that he had lost sight of. Jesus said, "You have answered correctly; do this and you will live." The lawyer had become so enamored with his knowledge of the word that it had become an end in itself. To "*do this*" was no longer part of the deal. Doing the word, or the *word becoming flesh* was not part of his worldview. It's no different today.

Consider how much power people can acquire by simply managing the right words. How many political leaders have gained positions of significant influence because of their mastery of a message? Sadly, way too many. Quite often, a good message coupled with a supporting media machine and money will trump character, competence and experience. What is true in the geopolitical world, rings even truer in the current state of Christendom. How many church leaders have become masters at doctrine, but are novices at demonstration? They can exegete scripture, but seldom encounter the purpose of scripture. How many Christians take pride in being called, 'word people,' or in going to a 'word church?' Is that really something to boast in? Of course, the Bible is central to our Christian faith, and it is our guide for all of life, but knowing the Bible without living the Bible is not real Christianity. It's not just for memorizing, it's for manifesting. The Holy Spirit inspired the Apostle John to write, "Don't love in word and tongue but by deed and truth" (1 John 3:18). The Apostle Paul wrote, "The Kingdom does not consist in words, but in power" (1 Corinthians 4:20). Just like a menu without good food is a bad restaurant, and promises without corresponding action is bad government, the message without miracles is not the ministry of Jesus. If the power of 'I love you' is in the 'loving' then the power of 'our healer' is in the 'healing,' and the power of 'our deliverer' is in the 'deliverance.' To tell people all about Jesus means showing them all about Jesus.

When Jesus said, "When you pray, pray like this.... your will be done on earth as it is in heaven," he had no exclusion clause. Meaning, our faith is real and relatable to all spheres of life. Jesus, through the power of the Holy Spirit, has come to have first place in everything. Whether you are an apostle or an astronaut, an evangelist or an engineer, a politician or a prophet, Jesus is your advantage in everything. This brings us to one of the bigger impediments to us translating our great salvation into daily experience, Gnosticism-dualism. It's a philosophy that separates our spiritual life from spheres of our natural/social life. To expose this lie and its effects, let's look at how Paul handled it.

Paul made an unusual apologetic to the believers in Rome. He said, "I am not ashamed of the gospel, for it is the power of God for salvation to everyone who believes" (Romans 1:16). Meaning, "I am not uncertain, insecure or inadequate in regards to this message." Now, why would Paul find it necessary to say that? Was this just a random, disconnected thought? The answer is no. If we back up just a bit, we find some context to his defensive comment. In verses

5-7 he mentions receiving an apostleship to bring about the obedience of faith among all the Gentiles. He then says, "Among whom you also are... to all who are beloved of God in Rome." Then in verse 13, he says that he does not want them to be unaware of how often he planned to come to them in Rome, but how he had been continually hindered. Then right before Paul says, "I am not ashamed" he writes, "I am eager to preach the gospel...in Rome." You can literally feel the emotion as he makes his case for wanting to be with them in Rome. What's going on here?

Paul was known as the apostle to the Gentiles. Yet in all his ministry travels he had not gone to Rome, the bastion of the Gentile world. A perception was emerging that maybe Paul was not as confident in the gospel's efficacy in Rome as he was in cities like Corinth or Ephesus. It would be easy for people to draw that conclusion. Paul represents the apostolic, the furthest reach of the kingdom, and he had gone everywhere except Rome. Paul not coming to Rome is being interpreted as a limitation. That's why Paul was unequivocal in his response, "For I am not ashamed of the gospel." He goes on to say, "For in it is the power of God for salvation for everyone ... for in it the righteousness of God is revealed." Righteousness merely is 'everything that is right about God.' Although Rome was seen as the 'big daddy' of human civilization and power, a place that could be quite intimidating, Paul was certain of the gospel's relevance and impact there. He was not confident because of his expertise in Roman culture, or because of his Roman citizenship, but because he was infected with everything that was right about God and it was contagious anywhere. Paul having to defend himself highlights the propensity to separate or compartmentalize the physical and the spiritual; the natural and the supernatural.

Generally speaking, dualism is the idea that in specific domains there are two sides or types. For example, in morality we have good and evil; in human design we have form and function; in time we have finite and infinite. Gnostic dualism is the separation or division of the natural and the spiritual. Gnosticism comes from the Greek word, 'gnosis,' which means knowledge. It taught that salvation was acquired through special knowledge and that God was too pure to have any contact with the material world. The early church was influenced by some of this gnostic teaching. The early Christian Gnostics refused to accept the bodily/physical resurrection of Jesus because they could not see the holy/divine (upper world) touching what flesh/physical (lower world) is. Gnosticism was the shunning of the material world. It created a conceptual divide between what is God's realm and what is man's realm. Today it's more commonly referred to as the 'sacred/secular divide.' Gnosticism attempts to rebuild the dividing wall that Jesus removed at Calvary. Although pure Gnostic-dualism is less common, a more subtle form creeps in through what I call 'hierarchies of preference.'

A hierarchy is defined as a ranking in order of importance. A 'hierarchy of preference' is where our current experiences with God become what we prefer, and then we view those preferences as more important to God. The fact is, certain behaviors, activities, and events do make us more 'God aware.' For example, we are more aware of the Holy Spirit's presence during our sensational worship on Sunday than during our science workshop on Monday. We feel him more in the prayer room than in the boardroom, and we trust him more on the mission field than on the sports field. Our degree of 'God awareness' can become the biggest hindrance to more. As wonderful as our level of God awareness may be, thank God that level is not the measure of where the Holy Spirit is or what the Holy Spirit does. God's presence and kingdom operate wherever there is faith.

Although David lived before the New Covenant, he understood and lived according to what I call the 'everywhereness of God's thereness.' In Psalm 139 David makes an observation that is life-changing. He wrote, "If I say, surely the darkness will overwhelm me, and the light around me will be night, even the darkness is not dark to you, and the night is as bright as the day, Darkness and light are alike to you." When I first read that scripture, it bothered me a bit. I thought it was putting darkness on equal terms with light. But then I realized what David was saying. He understood that no matter how dark it was around him, God was undiminished in his nature toward him. Once again Jesus is our quintessential model.

When Jesus was being arrested in the Garden of Gethsemane, Peter attempts to be heroic by drawing a sword and slicing off the ear of a slave named Malchus. Let's get the real picture of this moment. Rather than being lovingly heroic, Peter becomes savagely dramatic. He literally cuts off another person's body part. Malchus wasn't even one of the soldiers arresting Jesus, he was just an innocent bystander. Think about that. Peter had been walking with love incarnate for over three years. He was seen as the lead disciple among the twelve. Yet in one moment he goes from fisherman to gangster, from disciple to criminal. Unless you are a surgeon helping someone, cutting off a person's body part is usually a crime. That is about as dark as it gets. Movies, where body parts are being cut off, are usually called 'horror movies.' This was a horrible thing for Peter to do. Can you imagine what's going through the minds of the other disciples? I can hear John thinking, "Dude, you got serious issues!" In this very dark moment, what did Jesus do? He reaches forward and heals Malchus. That darkness did not, in any way restrict Jesus. Sometimes we forget that light shines in darkness; that no place is off limits to who Jesus is. Too many believers are allowing most of their experiences with Jesus to be postponed until heaven. Even the way we do church as an organization can feed dualistic tendencies.

In most church organizations there are lots of programs and activities that are part and parcel to being in that spiritual community. As necessary and beneficial as our church gatherings and activities are, they can be so emphasized and time-consuming that we unwittingly de-emphasize the rest of our everyday lives. We can get so busy applying our faith within the organization of the church that we hardly have time to do it in the trenches of daily life. As Christian leaders, we work tirelessly to get people into the support of Christian community. But what is meant to be supportive and complementary can become centralized and controlling. Our communities can become so insular that there is less and less relatability to the real world. Our thriving faith on Sunday downgrades to surviving faith on Monday. Jesus did not ask the Father to take us out of the world, but to keep us from the evil one (John 17:15). Even the way we approach the great commission can foster an unhealthy separation between ministry and daily life.

We quote the great commission as, "Go therefore and make disciples of all the nations." It sounds like something we do when we go on a mission trip to another region or country. What it really says is, "As you go, make disciples of all nations." In other words, as you do daily life make disciples. It's not just for the mission trip we take – it's for the journey of life we're on. God awareness in everyday life is imperative for converting hope into the experience. Paul was owned and operated by this truth. He told the Roman believers, "Since the creation of the world, His invisible attributes, His eternal power and divine nature have been clearly seen, being understood through what has been made" (Romans 1:20). The only way we can find a place where God is not, is by finding a place that has not been made. Meaning, anywhere you are is where he already is.

Francis Bacon, the developer of the scientific method, was credited with taking science from the contemplated to the practical. He said this, "We have two books laid before us to keep us from falling into error. First, the volume of scriptures, which reveal the will of God; then the volume of the creatures which express his power." One of the reasons why Christianity could give rise to great science is because men and women had God awareness in all of creation. All of creation is God's treasury waiting to be opened to men and women who act upon unrestricted faith in Jesus everywhere.

It's not rocket science. It's so simple that a child can understand it. When Dad calls home and tells his son or daughter that he is bringing ice cream, their first response is an excited "thank you, Daddy." Their next response is to run and meet Daddy as he comes up the driveway. Meaning, they believe it, and they act upon it. Whether Daddy does it with ice cream at home, a puppy at the mall or popcorn at the movie theatre, the response is the same: believing and receiving. When love leads it's not just a message, it's an experience.

5

You let love lead when you will try something new, and before anyone else does.

During part of my childhood, I lived in a house with a basement. Basements were more than just good storage places. In the American Midwest they also served as a refuge from possible tornados. Every once in a while I would decide to do a major cleaning of the basement. I was not asked to do it, nor was it part of a duty roster. With no prodding from my mom or the promise of reward, I would simply get motivated to do something productive – to improve the way the basement looked. Of course, this 'taking of initiative' was not always so noble or beneficial. I initiated my fair share of 'dumb.' Although my fallen nature, coupled with a moderate degree of insecurity, led me to do some stupid stuff, my inner drive to 'initiate' came from somewhere other than just fear, pride or lust. Taking the initiative, or wanting to improve something, no matter what others do or don't do, is part of our God-given design.

God, the 'first cause' of all creation, made us the 'first cause' of our own creations. The gift of our free will sets us apart from the rest of the animal kingdom. In giving us choice, God made us powerful. The choices we make in life range from comfortable and easy to uncomfortable and scary. Unfortunately or fortunately, depending on how you look at it, most growth and productivity is found in and around the uncomfortable to scary range. Another word that describes doing the uncomfortable or scary is 'risk.' It's where the outcome is uncertain and may result in loss or damage. Without risk-takers, we would not have airline travel, X-Games or a myriad of technological gadgets. There would be little to no development. Our decisions help make the impossible possible. When we take responsibility for our choices while embracing a lifestyle of risk, we change the world – we let love lead.

To be a 'first cause' implies a volitional ability beyond any conditions around us. Meaning, while our choices are influenced by what's in our environment, the environment does not determine our choices; we do. I often describe our free will as one of the best evidences that we are in the world, but not of the world – that we live in this place from a higher place. All animals are driven by instinct. There is a genetic pre-wiring in animals for almost everything they do. The salmon that swim upstream to spawn cannot choose to stop for reasons of self-preservation. They will die in the process. The migrating wildebeest cannot choose to avoid the river full of crocodiles. This pre-programming is not true of us.

We can make choices opposite the conditions around us. We can choose to do what's right regardless of the consequences. We can try something new with no guarantee of a positive outcome. This is the domain of faith. We can believe and act upon something merely because it's right or because it's a reasonable expression of who we are regardless of opposing factors. This is the seedbed of greatness. No one has ever demonstrated this as powerfully as Jesus.

Jesus said twelve words, (in the English translation) that changed the face of history. While being tortured to death and mocked, he uttered, "Father forgive them for they do not know what they are doing." At that moment Jesus demonstrated what living from heaven to earth really looks like. He revealed the power of free will in the face of contrary conditions. It's what the prophet Isaiah declared, "For behold, darkness will cover the earth and deep darkness the people, but my glory shall arise upon you" (Isaiah 60:2). Although he was rejected at the end of his life, he loved to the very end. His ability to forgive, under the most unforgivable conditions, caused heaven to slam into earth with a redemption that's unstoppable. Paul told the believers in Rome that Jesus is "the first born among many brethren" (Romans 8:29). The life Jesus modeled is our model for life. It's an ability to go through the darkness while still shining. It highlights the real nature of a believer's testimony: to be in the fiery furnace and not overheating; to be in a lion's den and not get eaten. What does this look like in the daily life of the believer? Its starts with personal responsibility. It's about responding from our resurrected nature rather than reacting from the fallen nature.

We are neither pre-programmed robots nor a bundle of irresistible emotions. We all have choice. At one time or another everyone has been victimized by the behaviors or actions of others. We have all been treated unfairly, and even cruelly. There are accidents and events in nature that we are powerless to avoid. Although at times, we have little control over what happens to us, we do have control over the responses from us. The writer of Proverbs captured how powerful this is when he wrote, "He who is slow to anger is better than the mighty, and he who rules his spirit, than he who captures a city" (Proverbs 16:32). Self-control is a fruit of the Spirit as well as the evidence of strong character. It is more powerful than we realize. Self-control or self-government is where most greatness springs from. I love how Hugo Grotius summed it up. He was a Dutch philosopher who systematized the law of nations. He wrote, "He does not know how to rule a kingdom if he cannot manage a province, nor can he manage a province if he cannot order a city, nor can he order a city if he cannot regulate a village, nor can he regulate a village if he cannot guide a family, nor can he guide a family if he cannot govern himself, nor can he govern himself unless his reason, will and appetite be ruled by God and wholly obedient to Him." There are few things more powerful than one person unmoved by anything but God and conscience. Winston Churchill called personal responsibility the "price of greatness." History and contemporary culture are replete with people who demonstrate the unstoppable force of living from the responsibility of their faith.

Abraham, not knowing where he was going, left his home for a place where God was the architect and builder (Hebrews

11:10). He would face life-threatening circumstances without wavering. No wonder he is called the 'father of faith.' Moses left the comforts of Pharaoh's house for the harsh conditions of a wilderness. Years later he marched back into Pharaoh's court with little more than a calling from God, a stick, and a stutter. His sole response to God led to an entire nation coming out of captivity. David, as a young shepherd, faced a seasoned warrior who was twice his size. While the army was standing back in fear, he ran to the battle line to meet Goliath. His faith became the foundation for his many exploits and the establishing of the Davidic kingdom. Peter calls out to Jesus who is walking on the water towards the boat, "Lord, if it is you, command me to come to you on the water" (Matthew 14:28). Jesus simply says, "Come," and Peter steps out of the boat and begins to walk on the water. Although Peter's first attempt at 'water walking' ended poorly, he acted against the grain of what's normal and raised the bar for living outside the box. These are just a few examples of what it looks like when we live from the inside-out.

No matter how many years we are in leadership, this 'growth formula' ingredient doesn't change. Connie and I have done many church plants in the United States and in South Africa. Each one required personal initiative and the willingness to risk. Our most recent church plant, Journey of Grace in Cape Town, South Africa, is no exception to that rule. In fact, it felt the most risky. We had just left a global organization and handed over our life's work. We felt a bit like Abraham – we knew where we couldn't stay, but we weren't sure where we were going. It felt like an experiment. We wanted to build a wineskin, a local church framework that was more favorable to the revival/kingdom culture values we were stewarding. We had a few people supporting us and many more criticizing us. It was scary, and it was risky, but we pressed in. The Holy Spirit gave us three directives: lean into Him, embrace the relationships that remain and do what He graced us to do. After a few years, we now have a thriving community of believers. We are seeing the fruit of taking initiative against the grain of the status quo. It's never easy, but it's always necessary, and it's forever a part of letting love lead.

Our ability to choose or take the initiative means that temporal circumstances cannot have the final say over our lives. Paul told the believers in Colossae that "Christ in them was the hope of glory" (Colossians 1:27). He also said that in Jesus are "hidden all the treasure of wisdom and knowledge" (Colossians 2:3). Those treasures are hidden in Christ, who is alive in us. To the degree that we take responsibility and take risks is the degree to which the stuff of heaven manifests through the stuff of us.

6

You let love lead when learning is as important as breathing.

We wouldn't refute the importance of learning any more than we would refute the necessity of breathing – yet we can take both for granted and miss the benefits. Each of us takes an average of 20,000 breaths per day, but many of us don't do it correctly and therefore become susceptible to illnesses, anxiety attacks, insomnia and depression. Short, shallow breathing only uses the top third of our lungs and leads to a poor exchange of oxygen and CO_2 in the bloodstream. This can leave anyone feeling anxious and fatigued. In like fashion, each of us has anywhere from 60,000 to 80,000 thoughts per day. Though this number is often criticized as mere speculation, the fact remains, the amount of information passing through our cerebral cortex is vast. Short, shallow thinking and learning uses very little of our cerebral capacity and leads to poor exchange for relationships and problem-solving. Question: Do we understand and embrace how vital learning is? Or are we just coasting along with a dusty, rusty cerebral database? Abraham Lincoln said that he did not think much of a man who was not wiser today than he was yesterday. In other words, daily learning is a qualifier for life and leading.

Learning, just like breathing, is a life source. To take our breathing metaphor one step further, the Apostle John wrote, "He breathed on them and said to them, 'Receive the Holy Spirit'" (John 20:22). The Hebrew word for Spirit is *Ruah,* and the Greek word is *Pneuma*. A predominant meaning and application for both is 'wind' or 'breath.' The Holy Spirit is the life and breath of God. The Holy Spirit is also called our teacher who leads and guides us into all truth. A Spirit-filled life, which is the very life-breath of God in His children, is the quintessential learning journey.

Solomon, who was considered the wisest man to ever live, said, "Give instruction to a wise man and he will be still wiser; teach a righteous man and he will increase his learning." Humility is the genesis of all virtues and the harbinger of all competence. Stephen Covey said, "When we are humble, teachable and open ... We can experience the paradigm shifts that open up the world to us." From their three-year research project, the authors of *Global Explorers* identified inquisitiveness as indispensable to effective leadership. They said, "Leaders are constantly curious and eager for knowledge." Kumar Birla, India's richest man, captured the essence of a learning mindset when he said, "Aggressively seek out learning ... know what you don't know, which skills you don't have and what you need to understand better." Lifelong learning is indispensable to good leadership and often inaccessible to bad leadership. Sir Winston Churchill candidly pointed out, "Personally I'm always ready to learn, although I do not always like being taught." What leads us to learning and what leads us astray?

President Harry Truman once said, "It's what you learn after you know it all that counts." Herein lies the secret to lifelong learning: knowing that you don't know, and prioritizing to learn what you don't know. One thing I discovered while doing my doctorate in strategic leadership is how little I knew about leadership. By the time I started working on the doctorate, I already had 25 years of leadership experience. Within no time I was confronted by how much there was to learn about leading. My most significant takeaway from the doctorate was not what I learned, but how to apply it and how to keep learning. Here is a clear and useful formula for learning. It comes from the acronym LEAD: listen, examine, apply and do it again.

Hearing and listening are not the same things. The former is simply the inner ear recognizing sounds and sending the information to the brain. The latter is an active process where we pay attention to that information for the purpose of understanding. A baby can hear the voice of their mother or father, but cognitive listening, which includes understanding, is not yet developed at that stage of life. Winston Churchill said that it takes as much courage to sit down and listen as it does to stand up and speak. We need the courage to listen because our defense mechanisms often war against good listening. This happens when we get overly protective of our opinions as well as overly critical of the people who are speaking. For both reasons, guts and grit are required for listening. The writer of Proverbs said, "Listen to me, and pay attention to my words" (Proverbs 7:24). Suspend judgment while they are speaking. Value their right to be heard, and remember, you can always learn something. Even if you don't agree with what they say, God defends their right to say it. Active listening leads to learning, and for that reason, there must be thoughtful examination.

Socrates said, "The unexamined life is not worth living." Socrates believed that personal and spiritual growth was the purpose of life. We are unable to grow without continuous examination of ourselves and the world around us. To examine simply means, "To look at something closely and carefully in order to learn more." A big part of the examination process is asking questions for the purpose of clarity and understanding. Most exams are a series of questions. The questions are designed to reveal your level of comprehension. Asking powerful questions is a key to learning. Albert Einstein said, "If I had an hour to solve a problem and my life depended on the solution, I would spend the first 55 minutes determining the proper question to ask, for once I know the proper question, I could solve the problem in less than 5 minutes." Jesus continually asked his disciples questions. Not because he didn't know, but because he wanted them to. Learn to ask more questions before drawing your conclusions. Then apply what you know. Einstein also said that all learning comes through experience.

Learning through experience is a well-known model in education. It was popularized by Kolb's 'experiential learning theory.' It's simply: have an experience, reflect and apply it. Confucius said, "I hear and I forget, I see and I remember, I do and I understand." Jesus gave us a similar model to follow. He did it, and they watched – they did it, and he watched. Applying what we have been taught is the key to an empowered life. Most education has a goal beyond the mere accumulation of knowledge. Who we become and what we do are the goal posts of learning. Then we 'do it again:' listen, examine and apply. It's not a seminar or a seven-year doctoral program, it's a journey. A journey that's often disrupted by the detours of ignorance, change and hubris.

Benjamin Franklin said, "We are all born ignorant, but one must work hard to remain stupid." It's hard to believe that grown-ups who have access to endless reams of information via high-speed internet technology are categorized as ignorant. Yet ignorance does abound. Often it's by choice. Ayn Rand stated it even stronger when she wrote, "The hardest thing to explain is the glaringly evident which everybody has decided not to see." One social behavior favoring the perpetuity of ignorance is 'group think.' Irving Janis coined the phrase in 1972 as a suitcase word for groups that make faulty decisions because of group pressure. The group is usually very insular, self-censoring and critical of differing viewpoints from outsiders. They maintain the illusion of unanimity, and they marginalize or even villainize those who leave the group. There are usually only one or a few within the group who determine what's acceptable. Some would classify this group as a 'cult.' Yet many Christians in ministry structures find themselves in varying degrees of 'group think' mode. One of the biggest contributors to 'group think' is when agreement is valued more than personal responsibility and conscience. This kind of ignorance is usually accompanied by hubris. It is the Achilles heel of leadership.

Writing for the Harvard Business Review, author and leadership consultant, John Baldoni wrote, "Like all vices, hubris is with us always. We all know bosses who believe it's their way or the highway. It is they who set the agenda, make the rules, determine all decisions, and never ever listen to alternate points of view. A leader's failure to solicit input from others due to an abiding sense of one's own infallibility is not a form of genius; it's a sign of stupidity. And like all forms of stupidity, the last one to recognize it is the one committing it." Pride and arrogance are equal opportunity vices. We are all susceptible to their seductions. They can cripple us on every front and without us even realizing it.

At different times, learning disabilities can afflict all of us. Whether from ignorance or pride, we can become resistant to new areas of learning. Peter Senge, founder and director of the Society for Organizational Learning identified seven learning disabilities. Among them is the disability of 'I am my position.' It's where we get defined by our role or job. Peter tells the story of an American steel company that was shutting down its plants in the 1980's. The company offered to train the steelworkers for new jobs. To their surprise, the workers chose unemployment and odd jobs, rather than training for new jobs. Later, a psychologist came in and discovered that the workers were suffering from an acute identity crisis. They could not see themselves as anything other than steelworkers. Here again is the issue of our identity or 'who we are.' We are all so much bigger and better than our careers or job descriptions. We are designed to be continuous learners by virtue of our heavenly designer who continues to express his eternal nature through us. That's why a passion for learning and an ongoing partnership with the Holy Spirit is paramount. No one and nothing can introduce us to ourselves like the Father, Son and Holy Spirit. We let love lead when we let ourselves love learning.

7

You let love lead when you can approach change and productivity like welcome friends rather than scary intruders.

I have been married to the same woman for over 36 years, but she has not been with the same man for those 36 years. Before you think poorly of Connie, let me explain. When I married Connie, she was secure, generous, courageous, passionate, smart, patient and full of the Holy Spirit. Yes, she has grown a lot, and she added more to her toolbox for life and living, but the wonderful person she was then is who she is today. That cannot be said of the man she married. Meaning, I had a lot more things that needed to change. Yes, I loved Jesus, her and people. I did have passion, courage and a calling, but I still carried a lot of brokenness from my past. I had quite a bit of fear dictating my behaviors and actions. I was impatient, reactive and selfish. Because I was pretty conscientious, I would usually repent quickly and try harder, but I had a lot of work to do over these 36 years. I had to embrace a journey of change. Whether in my personal capacity, my calling or just in day-to-day life, change could not be an option. To let love lead I had to approach change as a dear friend rather than a scary intruder.

Of course, we're talking about change for the better and not for the worse. The fact is, we seldom remain as we currently are. If we are not moving forward, we are usually falling backward. If we don't progress, we regress or digress. I play better on the guitar when I practice, I play worse when I don't. When I exercise, my fitness improves, when I don't, it diminishes. Even if our external context doesn't change (job, friends, income, education, housing, etc.), the condition of our soul usually does. If we don't cultivate a generous, kind and hopeful disposition, then a miserly, inconsiderate and cynical attitude is more likely to develop. Change is inevitable, but the nature of that change isn't. Productive change comes by design and from the decisions we make. Meaning, we have been created to be productive through our choices. When love is leading productive change is non-negotiable.

The Apostle John wrote, "I pray, that in all respects, you prosper and be in health as your soul does prosper" (3 John 2). John was inspired by the Holy Spirit to write that. We know that John is not praying that prayer for us. But someone else is. We are told in Hebrews 7:25 that Jesus always lives to make intercession for us. Jesus prays for our prosperity. He prays that we will gain in everything. Productivity is not just a goal – it is part of our essential design. Even our body chemistry is a stark reminder.

We have neurotransmitters like dopamine and endorphins. Dopamine or the 'feel good' hormone is essential to motivation. It has also been called the 'reward drug.' Dopamine is associated with the pleasure system of the brain, providing feelings of enjoyment and reinforcement to motivate a person proactively to perform certain activities. When we study hard and pass an exam, we are rewarded emotionally and motivated to study more. When we surprise ourselves by running farther and faster than the day before, dopamine motivates us to do it again. Endorphins are known as a natural analgesic. They reduce the pain of stressful conditions and activities. The 'runner's high' is attributed to endorphins. They assist us in persevering through the pain and discomfort of difficult moments. Most productivity is found on the other side of our current comfort levels. Advancing in life is seldom comfortable and is always the domain of change. Although we know this, we often make choices contrary to a growthpath. What hinders productive change and what are some essential areas for change?

I believe that fear is one of the greatest hindrances to change that leads to productivity. Those who have excelled the most have given in to fear the least. Fear is as common as air. Not all fear is bad and to be rejected. For example, the fear of the Lord is the beginning of wisdom and prolongs life. (Proverbs 9:10 and Proverbs 10:27). This Hebrew word for 'fear' is *yare*. In our relationship to God, it means to revere, to hold in high esteem, to respect, to stand in awe of. In Satan's accusation of Job to God, he said, "Does Job fear God for nothing (Job 1:9)?" This word for 'fear' is yare, which means reverence and respect. Later, when Job was lamenting his terrible condition, he said, "For what I fear comes upon me, and what I dread befalls me" (Job 3:25). He was using the Hebrew word *pachad*, which means "to be in dread of." We fear God from a position of awe, reverence and respect, but we are not to be afraid of Him because of impending punishment or doom. Another positive application of fear relates to self-preservation. Leonardo Da Vinci said, "Just as courage imperils life, fear protects it." Meaning, we don't walk across the street when cars are coming, and we don't get out of our car in a lion park. A healthy fear of harmful consequences is necessary to keep our stupid-quotient to a minimum.

The fear that we must resist at all times comes from our adversary and the domain of darkness, and it seeks to move our beliefs, behaviors and actions away from faith and obedience. Contrary to a popular notion, "fear not" was not placed in the Bible 365 times to cover every day of the year. It's closer to 80 times, and a bit more when considering other ways to say it. But the fact remains, "fear not" is a directive from God to his people. The Apostle Paul told Timothy that God has not given us a spirit of fear, but of power, love and a sound mind (2 Timothy 1:7). Fear is not from God. Fear is only valid where God is absent, but in regards to the life of a believer, no such place exists. The Apostle John was unequivocal when he said, "There is no fear in love; but perfect love casts out all fear, because fear involves punishment, and the one who fears is not perfected in love" (1 John 4:18). What often goes unnoticed is what John wrote before that. He said that "love is perfected with us...because as he is, so also are we in the world" (verse 17). Did you hear that? Jesus is exceptional, but he is not the exception. Meaning, his nature in the earth is our nature in the earth. Just as the enemy had nothing in him, the enemy has nothing in us. This highlights the issue of identity. Knowing who he is and who we are is essential to resisting paralyzing fear and embracing ongoing, productive change. Although much can be said about our identity, for the purpose of embracing change we need to see our own lives through the lens of 'more' or 'better.' To settle for mediocrity in anything is to remain way below who we are and who Jesus is in us. Since we are talking about change for the purpose of productivity, I will highlight three essentials for productivity.

In his book, *Seeing Organizational Patterns*, Robert Keidel argues that all organizational productivity is a partnership and balance between three elements. He talks about triangular thinking, where organizations are inherently triadic because there are only three ways that people can relate to each other without conflict: autonomy, cooperation and control. For example, starting a new business will require a distinct service or product, collaboration between various stakeholders and appropriate management structures. All three of these will go through necessary adjustments and upgrades to keep up with changes in the environment and to improve the business. In our personal growth, these three need equal consideration.

Whether we are improving ourselves physically, relationally, educationally, vocationally, financially or spiritually our person, our partnerships and our structures need change. Connie and I recently relocated our USA base to Gallup, New Mexico. We are spending six months of the year serving a church called the Lighthouse. Our primary focus is building a team and growing the community of believers. To be successful, and because the conditions are very different from our home in Cape Town, South Africa, we had to add to our knowledge base, establish new connections and create new structures. This formula can be applied to any area of productive change. If you find yourself hitting the ceiling spiritually, ask yourself three questions: What am I neglecting in my walk with Jesus? Who can help me to improve? What new disciplines do I need to put into place?

One of the most encouraging and motivating reminders is that today can be better than yesterday, and tomorrow better than today. We don't have to stay stuck in any area of our personal lives or vocations. Even when we find ourselves in the whirlwind of so much uncertainty, Paul tells us that God causes all things to work together for our good (Romans 8:28). Deepak Chopra noted, "All great changes are preceded by chaos." Embrace your journey of change and watch productivity be your daily reward.

8

You let love lead when you are quick to apologize and the last to criticize.

One of my favorite illustrations that Jesus used with his disciples is the 'log and the speck.' It is a brief, but powerful reminder of how to keep our focus and efforts in the right place. He said, "Why do you look at the speck in your brother's eye, but you do not notice the log that is in your own eye" (Matthew 7:3). Jesus then says, "First take the log out of your own eye, and then you will see clearly to take the speck out of your brother's eye" (Matthew 7:5). We know that the log is a metaphor for something else. No one can have a physical log in their eye. The key here is the difference in size. A log is a whole lot bigger than a speck. Meaning, we should be working on ourselves a heck of a lot more than we are working on someone else. Jesus is saying that clarity to help others comes from the priority of dealing with ourselves first and continually. Being quick to apologize and the last to criticize is about better self-reflection. When aiming at the jugular of someone else's bad attitude or poor behavior, we often run right past our own. I had an eye-opening experience many years ago that highlights this very point.

I was driving in the city of Johannesburg – down a road where the traffic lights were not synchronized. This meant getting caught at every red light for the next few miles. As I was waiting for a traffic light to turn green a white BMW came past me at high speed. It was was apparent to me that the driver was trying to make it to the next light before it turned red. I found myself slightly irritated by the driver of that BMW. When I caught up to the car, which had been stopped by the next red light, I was surprised to find a lady in the driver's seat. When the light turned green, she took off like a Formula One driver. In an attempt to catch the next green light she drove recklessly around other cars. Once again she was not successful, and by this time I am really bugged. Her aggressive driving now had my full and undivided attention. I found myself looking and praying for a traffic officer who would witness her vehicular insanity and then take appropriate punitive action.

I came to a point in the road where I found myself in a dual turning lane right next to the BMW. As I looked in my rearview mirror, I saw the answer to my prayers, a traffic officer. At this point, I am hoping, almost praying that this female drag racer will continue her reckless behavior. Then to my utter joy, she speeds off without having the right-of-way. After a few seconds I gained the right-of-way and turned in the same direction, suddenly I heard the police siren. By this time I am almost ecstatic at the thought of this 'vehicle vixen' getting the full penalty for her crimes. As I glance once more in my rearview mirror, to my utter shock, this purveyor of road justice was pulling me over. I pulled off to the side of the road and waited in disbelief as the traffic officer approached my car. As I rolled down the window, I was stunned to hear the nature of my crime. The officer said, "You neglected to use your turning signal." My first thought was, "That lady is going to kill someone, and you're on me about my turning signal." Well, the next voice I heard was the Holy Spirit. He said, "It's not the big issue in someone else's life that will pull you off the road of your destiny, it's the small stuff that you neglect in your own life that will." It's very easy to get distracted by the problems of others and neglect the ones closer to home. Paul said, "I buffet my body and I make it my slave, lest after I preach to others I may be disqualified" (1 Corinthians 9:27).

The point is not about turning a blind eye to other people's problems, especially in our significant relationships, but it is about starting with ourselves. When we expect from others what we don't practice at home, we miss growth opportunities, attract a spirit of hypocrisy and open the door for mistrust and cynicism. We find an interesting dialogue between Jesus and Peter (John 21). While Jesus was dealing with Peter about his own heart, Peter turns around and sees John following them and says, "What about this man?" In an effort to deflect attention away from himself, Peter brought up John. Jesus' response was quick and precise, "What is that to you? You follow me." Meaning, don't use someone or something else as a red herring. Don't get distracted from what God is doing in your heart. Famous author, G.K. Chesterton was asked, along with other prominent writers, to participate in an essay writing contest. The essay had to answer the question, "What is wrong with the world?" His entire essay consisted of, "Dear Sirs, What is wrong with the world? I am. Yours Sincerely, G.K. Chesterton." Imagine how much better the world would be if everyone lived by the truth of Chesterton's response. This commonsense approach is so simple, and yet very elusive to so many.

The amount of criticism and deflection flying around at any given moment is as numerous as the sand. We cannot read a newspaper or listen to a news channel without scathing attacks against this group or against that leader. So many conversations are nothing but criticism and blame shifting. The judicial system is choked with attackers and defenders. No place seems immune to this virus of accusations and incriminations. It's frightening how quickly people will believe a negative report about someone they don't know. Even if the facts are correct, often the spirit behind those facts is not. When love is leading, the spirit of accusation and strife is not. When love is leading, we refuse to be baited into being easily offended. When love is leading, we address a problem from a spirit of gentleness and humility. When love is leading, building someone up is the goal, rather than tearing them down. When love is leading, we hear someone's heart before rendering judgment. Even when someone is wrong Paul said, "Brethren, even if someone is caught in any trespass, you who are spiritual, restore such a one in a spirit of gentleness..." (Galatians 6:1).

Most of us have been a perpetrator as well as a victim. We

have drawn conclusions about someone without knowing all the facts, and we have had judgments made about us without the whole story being known. Either way, the spirit of that is unloving and unhealthy. There are few things that grieve the Holy Spirit like the spirit of accusation attacking the very people Jesus died for. Paul told the believers in Galatia that if they walk by the Spirit, they will not carry out the desires of the flesh (Galatians 5:16). The flesh that Paul is referring to is found in the preceding verse. He said, "But if you bite and devour one another, take care that you are not consumed by one another" (verse 15). Biting and devouring one another is a metaphor for tearing people up with our words and then feeding on the damage done. The cannibalizing of the Body of Christ has many disguises, but they all have the same outcomes: diminishing people, destroying relationships and tarnishing the testimony of Jesus through the church.

Even if we have all the facts, until we hear someone's heart, or at least have the right spirit, we won't have the truth. James tells us that "the wisdom from above is first pure, then peaceable, gentle, reasonable, full of mercy…" (James 3:17). A spirit of accusation has none of these qualities. It is full of distortions, exaggerations and self-justifications. When we let love lead our port-of-entry is our own soul. We enter everything from the vantage point of 'examining ourselves' and 'building up one another.' When love leads Jesus is glorified, people are edified and the Kingdom of God advances.

9

You let love lead when being challenged and corrected is actually sought after.

Many years ago, I arrived at a Sunday service where I was scheduled to speak. I was greeted at the front entrance by some friendly people. After entering the building, I was greeted by some ushers. Then I entered the auditorium and exchanged greetings with several people as I walked to the front. On arriving at the front I was greeted by the pastor. Immediately after the greeting, he took me aside and told me that I had toilet paper hanging off my face. To my utter surprise and mild embarrassment, I had forgotten about the wadded-up piece of toilet paper I had applied to a cut I received while shaving. That small rolled-up piece of toilet paper had unraveled and was now dangling about two inches off my face. That pastor was my new best friend. What struck me as odd was how many people saw it and said nothing. Honestly, I would have been so much happier if the first person I met had pointed it out. When love leads being challenged and corrected is really appreciated.

I am not suggesting that it should or will feel good when flaws or mistakes are pointed out. The first thing I felt was embarrassment. But I was very thankful for someone being honest with me. Of course, receiving something deeply corrective is much more challenging; especially when we are leaders. I have been corrected by people more times than I can count – even by those who have been wrong in their assessment and correction. But the richness of my life is the better Christian, husband, father, leader and friend I am becoming because of it. I understand and appreciate other people showing me what I can't see or won't see. A friend of mine once said, "We can put a man on the moon, but we can't see the back of our own necks." God designed us to need each other. Our personal choices are the most essential first-causes towards a preferable future, but the input of others is equally essential for getting us there.

Later, in 'who we are together,' we will look at the nature of our relationships. The focus here is simply embracing our need for correction and pursuing it. There are many benefits experienced through different relationships, but without openness to correction, we are likely to miss out on many of them. Solomon, one of the wisest men who ever lived, said, "Reprove a wise man and he will love you" (Proverbs 9:8). He also said, "Reprove one who has understanding and he will gain knowledge" (Proverbs 19:25). It takes some understanding to turn a reproof into a blessing.

First, it's as simple as children learning in school. From all the exercises and activities they participate in, to the teacher's ongoing feedback, a child faces correction all the time. Young children are usually very receptive to correction. They are not nearly as defensive as adolescents. We get much more defensive as we get older. Children are less self-conscious, and therefore they don't fear mistakes like adults. They don't correlate mistakes to rejection. Who they are is not yet wrapped up in how much they know or how well they do. That is a learned behavior, which unfortunately comes later. Jesus did say, "Unless you are converted and become like little children, you will not enter into the kingdom of heaven" (Matthew 18:3). Remaining comfortable with the feedback, challenge and correction from others is a healthy childlike quality we all need.

Second, without feedback from those more experienced, we can't get an accurate picture of where we are. I learned this the hard way while attending High School. I was a wrestler. Actually, I was a very accomplished wrestler. There was a tournament that I was competing in. This was in Memphis, Tennessee. It was the Cotton Carnival Freestyle Wrestling Tournament. Just before the tournament, Olympic Champion, Wayne Wells was doing a wrestling clinic for us. Since I was in his weight class, he used me to demonstrate different wrestling moves and techniques. At the end of the clinic, he asked if I would like to wrestle some. I gladly took the challenge. Within three seconds I took him down and put him on his back. The emotional exhilaration of that moment was like nothing I had ever felt before. To put an Olympic champion on his back in front of hundreds of people made me feel godlike. My soul was screaming out to this Olympic champion, 'Who's your daddy.' Unfortunately or fortunately, depending on how you look at it, my exalted moment only lasted for a few seconds. He immediately reversed me and put me on my back. He had me in a wrestling hold where I could not breathe, and he knew it. He held me there just long enough to remind me who daddy was. There were several lessons I learned from that moment. One in particular was the need for an accurate assessment of my ability. Well, I got that accurate assessment – and it took someone better than me to provide it.

How many of us are around leaders who are more experienced, more mature or more successful? If we are, do we make a conscious effort to get their input? I have discovered two glaring impediments in this regard. Either, we don't access leaders who have more experience or maturity, or when we do, we are so busy maintaining the appearance of strength and success that we don't leave any room for receiving. Insecurity and naivety have a way of blocking access to the challenges and adjustments we so desperately need. Everyone, regardless of accomplishments in life, need the grace and input that comes when we humble ourselves before God and others. David J Bobbs in his article entitled, *Benjamin Franklin, George Washington, and the Power of Humility in Leadership* wrote, "Of all virtues vital for leadership, humility elicits the most lip service – and the least decisive action. It's a hard-won virtue, constantly demanding an honest assessment of our own merit. Humility asks us to acknowledge our imperfections. It requires that we admit when we are wrong and then change course." Humility, far from being a soft and deferring disposition, is the strength of a yielded heart to God and truth. Humility is not an emotion; it's a disposition and a practice. It's as simple as paying attention rather than being the center of attention. It appreciates challenge and embraces correction. Real humility can receive from someone whether they are more experienced or not.

As leaders, we should be on the receiving and giving end of challenge and correction. Personally, I am privileged to walk with some veteran leaders. Although many of them are my peers, they carry insights and experience that I don't have. I know that I need their feedback and challenge. It takes real vulnerability to let others peer review your work. I find that asking questions and running scenarios by them is very helpful. Many of the successes I've gained and blunders I've avoided came from their sobering responses. Honestly, I wish I had done this more. Most of us, at one time or another, have allowed fear or pride to get in the way of - 'crisis-averting' feedback. Because of the fear of being controlled many people refuse to let others get that close. It's one of the biggest mistakes we will make in leadership. How many disasters could be avoided if we would only listen better? How many victories are as close as the next challenge and correction? Many, I am sure. When love is leading, challenge and correction are a part of succeeding. If you don't have peers or leaders in your life that you can do this with, find some. It will save your life.

10

You let love lead when you will get up after continually being knocked down.

About 5 years ago, Connie and I made a life-changing decision. We left the global organization that we had been part of for over 25 years. It was our life work in South Africa. The people in the organization were our closest friends and spiritual family. To make a long story very short, we knew that we were called to build differently, and after lots of agonizing prayer, we handed in our resignation. Honestly, it was by far the most painful thing we have ever done. Unlike Peter, when we first stepped out of the boat we didn't walk on the water. Of course, Peter did start going under before Jesus took hold of him. Well, we seemed to go under from our first step. I am not saying that Jesus didn't have hold of us, but it felt like we were drowning in pain and uncertainty. We lost most of our relationships, and we were having to start over.

We had no ministry structure and very little income. Just when we thought we were out of the game and on the bench, Jesus hands us the ball and puts us back in the game. During the lowest point of our Christian lives, the Holy Spirit led us to do a new church plant. While battling intense emotional pain we got up and did what Jesus said to do. When love is leading, you can get up after one of the worst knockdowns ever.

Knockdowns come in all shapes and sizes. They result from good decisions and bad decisions. They are unavoidable. We will all get flattened by something. It will knock the wind out of our sails, the peace out of our souls and friends out of our lives. Getting knocked down is among our worst and best moments. I love what Nelson Mandela said, "Do not judge me by my successes, judge me by how many times I fell down and got back up again." Falling down is part of our humanity and getting back up is our connection to divinity. As the writer of Proverbs reminds us, "For a righteous man falls seven times, and rises again" (Proverbs 24:16).

Few people have modeled being knocked down and getting back up quite like the Apostle Paul. He told the believers in Corinth, "Are they servants of Christ...I more so; in far more labors, in far more imprisonments, beaten times without number, often in danger of death. Five times I received from the Jews thirty-nine lashes. Three times I was beaten with rods, once I was stoned, three times I was shipwrecked, a day and a night I have spent in the deep" (2 Corinthians 11:22-25). In Acts 14 we have the account of Paul getting stoned. It says, "But the Jews came from Antioch and Iconium, and having won over the crowds, they stoned Paul and dragged him out of the city, supposing him to be dead" (Acts 14:19). The implication here is that Paul was stoned to death. Many Bible commentators connect Paul getting caught up into the third heaven to this stoning experience. After Paul is stoned, the scripture says, "But while the disciples stood around him, he got up and entered the city" (Acts 14:20). Except for the resurrection of Jesus, this was the 'mother' of all getting up. Think about it; he had just been pummeled with stones and rocks – to the point of death. His body was bruised and bloodied. In spite of his battered state, the next day he travels with Barnabas to Derbe and preaches the gospel. I can see the hordes of hell shrieking at the sight of Paul's strength in such weakness.

Another herculean 'getting up' is found in the life of David. When David and his men returned to Ziklag, they found it was overthrown, burned with fire and all their families taken captive by the Amalekites. It said that David and his men wept until there was no strength left in them. That is a whole lot of crying. To make matters worse, the men spoke of stoning David. After being knocked to the canvas by this tremendous loss it says, "But David strengthened himself in the Lord" (1 Samuel 30:6). Herein lies the secret to always getting up no matter what: being strengthened in the Lord. Since God is love and love never fails, and God is in us, we will prevail no matter how much we fail. Failure can never have the final say over our lives. This is part of the testimony of our life of faith: being in a earth-destroying flood and thriving; being too old to have children and becoming the father and mother of a multitude; being in a fiery furnace and walking around; or, being tortured to death and rising from the dead.

When love leads staying down is never an option.

Whether we are a Christian or not, there is wiring in each of us that refuses to give up. The raw material of greatness germinates as we push against the pull of loss or failure. We will not stay down. Some friends of mine, Andy and Eve McGibbon told me a story about their son, Matthew. When Matthew was around five years old, they went to visit some friends. Their friends owned a big Rottweiler. These dogs can be quite dangerous. Unbeknownst to the grownups, little Matthew had made his way over to this big dog. As Andy and Eve were chatting with their friends, they hear this dog snarl and snap ferociously. They turned to see little Matthew under the body of this big dog. They rushed to his rescue. The dog had pounced on Matthew, and it looked horrifying. As they grabbed hold of him and began examining him for bite marks, he stands straight up, points at the dog and says, "I'm gonna kill that dog." While his parents are fearing the effects of such trauma, little Matthew shows them just how tough we really are. This is one reason why a rescuing mentality can be so detrimental. We all need opportunities to fight our way back. Every time we bounce back, we get stronger, and we rise higher. Yes we need nurturing and support, but we don't need coddling and sheltering. Especially when the fall or failure is self-inflicted.

It can be much more difficult bouncing back from falls or failures that are of our making. Honestly, when the loss is my own fault, I tend to beat myself up over and over again. The battle against guilt, shame or condemnation is as tough as it gets. There is only one remedy; you choose to rise up by faith in the one who rose up for you. You look into the face of your heavenly Father who meets you at that choice. Then you let the words of the Father answer the accusations against you, "Quickly bring out the best robe and put it on him, and put a ring on his hand and sandals on his feet....for this son of mine was dead and has come to life again..." (Luke 15:22-24). You are alive and clothed in his righteousness. Your worth, your works and your walk is as if you had never sinned. When love leads, we can't stay down because the one who lives in us always picks us up.

PART II

WHO OTHERS ARE

11

You let love lead when people who work with you feel valued.

How many people know who Hobab was? He was Moses' brother-in-law. In Numbers 10 we find a brief and interesting dialogue between Moses and Hobab. Moses says to Hobab, "We are setting out to the place of which the Lord said, "I will give it to you," come with us and we will do you good." To that request Hobab responds, "I will not come, but rather I will go to my own land and relatives." Then Moses alters the request by saying, "Please do not leave us, inasmuch as you know where we should camp in the wilderness, and you will be as eyes for us." Although not stated in the text, we know that Hobab must have agreed to journey with them because his descendants are mentioned in the Book of Judges as living in Canaan. What stands out is that Hobab only decided to travel with them after Moses expressed their need for him. In his previous request, Moses only mentioned their benefit to him. It was Moses' value for Hobab rather than Hobab's need for Moses that won Hobab's heart. We all need to feel valued by others. It is a primary motivator and driver. There are several criteria that determine and communicate value. Consider how value is ascribed to a particular product. Factors like, its purpose, the cost to produce it, the price to purchase it, who created it and supply and demand all factor into its intrinsic and extrinsic value.

First, we all have a purpose. In general, our purpose is the reason for our existence. From a biblical, Christian worldview, our purpose is to know God and make him known. It's to experience God and reveal him in all of life. Paul told the believers in Corinth, "Whether, then, you eat or drink or whatever you do, you do to the glory of God" (1 Corinthians 10:31). More specifically, that purpose unfolds through the many things we do and experience in life. Although our value is determined by God, our awareness of personal value is connected to how we function and contribute in different relationships. Simply put, we see and experience our value as we add value in relationships.

I discovered this by accident when I first became a Christian. On September 17, 1979, I prayed to receive Jesus as my Lord and Savior. There was a Christian fellowship called Maranatha at the University I was attending. A friend of mine who had become a Christian a few months earlier introduced me to Stuart Small, who was the pastor of the Christian fellowship. He shared a short gospel message with me, and I took the plunge. It was a life-transforming experience on every level. In one moment, a God I never knew became my heavenly father and a group of strangers became my spiritual family. To this day I will never forget them asking me if I would help set up chairs for the Sunday morning service. It happened within the first few days of becoming a Christian. What seemed so mundane on the surface actually pulled my heart towards this new community of people. They asked me to be the 'chairman' of the church. Seriously, to be trusted with something as simple as setting up chairs made me feel valued. I have made this a practice in my own ministry ever since. I love for people to have opportunities to contribute as soon as possible. The sooner they can see their value in practical ways, the better. This is one of the keys to having a Body of leaders rather than just a few leaders in the Body.

Second, if you were purchasing a Ferrari, it would be much more expensive than a Volkswagen Beetle. The higher price tag of the Ferrari is one of the indicators of better quality and value. What was the price tag for you and me? Paul told the believers in Corinth to glorify God in their bodies because they were bought with a price (1 Corinthians 6:20). After calling together the elders from the church of Ephesus, he said, "Be on guard for yourself and for all the flock, among which the Holy Spirit has made you overseers, to shepherd the church of God which he purchased with his own blood (Acts 20:28). Honestly, the fact that the lifeblood of Jesus was the price paid for each of us is difficult to comprehend. I remember seeing the price for a particular guitar and thinking, "Wow, should I play it or should I worship it." The price tag told me that this was an exceptional guitar. Well, that 'wow' belongs to every person on the planet. From the prisoner on death row to the CEO of a Fortune 500 company the price was the same, his lifeblood. Our lives cost God the life of his son. Nothing in all of creation is as valuable as one soul.

Third, my daughter Melody made me a coffee cup in her art class at school. She was only 8 years old at the time. We had a lot of coffee cups in our cupboard. All of them were better made and prettier, but none of them had my heart like that cup. I would not have sold it for $1000.00. After she gave me the coffee cup, I did not want to use any other. I stopped using our other cups. It was special because Melody made it. Her hands had shaped the clay and painted "I Love Dad" on it. When I held that cup, I was holding a part of her. When we moved our house from Johannesburg, South Africa, to Nashville, Tennessee it did not get packed. I looked everywhere for it. When I went back to South Africa I asked if anyone had seen it. I never did find it, and I've never forgotten how the work of her hands became so valuable to me. Similarly, we have all been handmade by God. We are not just lucky mud that clawed its way out of the primordial soup. We are all fearfully and wonderfully made by God and in his image. He created a universe and a planet as the staging for the apex of his creation, you and me.

Finally, when something is rare, or a one of a kind, it's usually much more valuable. Unique and special qualities will cause its value to skyrocket. Gems like the Koh-I-Noor diamond and paintings like the Mona Lisa are considered priceless. The rarity and quality of these items attract a tremendous amount of fame and adoration. In 2014 alone, 9.3 million people visited the Louvre in France where the Mona Lisa is on display. The former director of the Louvre, Henri

Loyrette, believes that 80% of those people came only to see the Mona Lisa. As beautiful as the Mona Lisa is, it doesn't hold a candle to how rare and special we are. In a population of seven billion people, no two people are alike. Consider this, your body is a temple of the Holy Spirit, your soul is a vehicle for the fullness of God and your spirit will live forever. Nothing in all of creation is as unique as you and me. Every time you see someone, you see a one-of-a-kind masterpiece. You are looking at a miracle. Author and consultant, Dr. Ali Binazir looked at all the things that would have to happen for you or me to exist. He showed that the probability of our existence without a miracle (divine intervention) is nonexistent. It would be equivalent to 2,500,000 people each having a dice with a trillion sides – then throwing their dice at the same time and coming up with the same number. Each of us is a miracle designed to release more miracles. Nothing in all of creation can do what God created people to do. Paul said, "For the anxious longing of creation waits eagerly for the revealing of the sons of God....that the creation itself also will be set free from its slavery to corruption into the freedom of the glory of the children of God" (Romans 8:19-21). We are designed to unlock the treasures of creation, and understanding of our value serves that end.

Ask the Holy Spirit to help you to see people the way he does. Each person is so much more than their gender, their age, their ethnicity, their educational or economic status, their role or vocation, or their good and bad behaviors. When we let love lead, we get heaven's perspective of people, and then people get motivated by how valuable they really are.

12

You let love lead when people's mistakes cause you to encourage them even more.

If there is one thing I have learned about following Jesus, he is not put off by our shortcomings, mistakes or failures. Personally, I have discovered more of his mercy and grace in times of weaknesses than in times of strength and productivity. Since Jesus is our model, how do we respond when confronted with the mistakes of others? Do we keep them at arm's length until they get their act together or do we just commiserate in their mess? When love leads we can give to others in their weakest moments.

Much of life is lived in the tension between need and provision. It is a love-hate relationship. Being extremely thirsty is unpleasant, but drinking cool water is much more satisfying when we are. No one likes the feeling of extreme hunger, but eating is much more fun when we are. Personally,

I hate when my back itches, but when my wife is around I actually love it. Because the itchiness makes her scratching my back feel heavenly. This juxtaposition between need and supply is a big part of our walk with Jesus. This is part of the magic of the song *Amazing Grace*. When you know you are lost, getting found is life-altering. Anyone who receives their sight after being blind will value seeing much more than those who have always had it. Let's take a closer look at how Jesus processes our weakness.

In John 8, we find Jesus teaching in the Temple. Some Pharisees and Scribes bring a woman to him. She had been caught in the act of adultery. They remind him that the Law of Moses commands that she be stoned, and then they ask him what he thinks. He immediately drops to the floor and begins writing on the ground. Before continuing with what Jesus was doing on the ground, it must be noted that what these Pharisees were doing was extremely dark. These religious leaders were posturing themselves on the back of the woman's shame and pain, and for no other reason than to accuse Jesus. There are few things morally darker than using the rubble of someone's brokenness to make us look good. Sadism is defined as taking pleasure in the pain of another. In this sadistic moment, Jesus goes to ground.

Why did Jesus leave his seat and go to the ground? Was it because he had something to write and he didn't have a whiteboard handy? The primary reason Jesus got on the floor was because the woman was there. He met her in the lowest place. It was hard and dirty. He met her in the mess of her life. The first and best evidence of Jesus' compassion is not in removing a mess, but in meeting someone in their mess.

The fact that Jesus shows up in the problem is far more revealing and liberating than the problem being solved. How Connie and I stand with each other through tough times says much more about the character of our love than how we stand in good times. Jesus meets her in her shame and pain, then he begins to write.

What was Jesus writing? I have heard some interesting answers to that question. Some have suggested that Jesus was writing down the sins of the Pharisees. I've even heard a few preachers say that he was inscribing the names of their mistresses. As funny as these answers may be, it's very bad theology. Meaning, Jesus does not overcome shame by shaming. The question we should be asking isn't, "What is Jesus writing, but, what is Jesus doing?" Jesus is actually modeling a new creation moment.

In Genesis 1:2 we find similar darkness. It says, "And the earth was formless and void, and darkness was over the surface of the deep..." The Hebrew word for darkness here is *khoshek*. It is moral darkness rather than a physical one. It means, ignorance, misery, sorrow, death and wickedness. This was the state of the world before the Spirit began to move and bring forth creation. How did God create Man? He stooped down into time, space and matter. He got down in the dirt and formed mankind from the dust of the ground. In like fashion, Jesus wrote in the dirt on the ground. The word 'wrote' is *grapho*, and it means to carve out, to reshape or reform. This is a new creation moment. Only Jesus can step into our darkness and shape a brand new life.

Why did Jesus stoop down and straighten up twice? And why did he say, "He who is without sin, cast the first stone?"

Jesus asking that question of the religious leaders was not to shame them. He was showing them that they were on the ground with her. Meaning, if they threw stones at her, they would be throwing stones at themselves. He meets all of us in our messes. He was in the dirt with the adulterous woman and the Pharisees. Jesus stooped down and straightened up the first time to meet her where she was, and he stooped down and straightened up the second time to make sure she didn't stay there. Jesus will meet us where we are, but he won't leave us there. That is the model we have with Jesus.

We should never turn away from people with problems, and we should never shy away from directing people towards solutions. Leadership at its finest is helping others move from one place to a more improved place. Having empathy and compassion is essential, but encouraging and equipping people towards personal responsibility and growth is non-negotiable. Jesus did not come to just 'seek' the lost – he came to 'seek and save' the lost. He did not come as a diagnostician to just point out the illness, he came as a physician to heal the sick. He is more than a spiritual hospice, providing comfort in our troubles, he is the answer to our troubles.

Herein lies the real joys of leadership: helping someone advance their life in one way or another. Connie and I have seen hundreds of people move their lives out of spiritual death, emotional bondage, physical illness, economic devastation and relational carnage. We have witnessed depression defeated, cancers healed, poverty removed and marriages restored. No matter how bad it is, like Job, we will declare and experience, 'our Redeemer lives.'

13

You let love lead when others want you to lead even more than you want to.

I t's been said that the best evidence of a good leader is found among his or her followers. How people respond to a leader is often more valuable than the knowledge, skill or experience the leader may possess. History is replete with talented leaders who lost the trust of others and forfeited their ability to influence. Why people trust and follow certain leaders has an enormous effect on the nature of any partnership. Was leadership taken by the most forceful personality, the smoothest communicator, the quickest decision maker or the most prominent financial giver? Or was it given to a servant-leader by the confident consent of informed and responsible followers? When love leads the latter is the norm. You won't have to find followers because they find you. This is what happened to David after he fled from Saul. His only ambition was to serve the King and the nation of Israel, but Saul's insecurity turned him against David. After David came to the cave of Adullam, it says that his brothers and all his father's household went to him. 1 Samuel 22:2 reads, "And everyone who was in distress, and everyone who was in debt, and everyone who was discontented, gathered to him; and he became captain over them."

The word 'gathered' comes from a root word that means, 'To grasp.' David did not just take leadership, rather, they took him as their leader. He simply said 'yes' to what they gladly gave. Because David had lost everything and was on the run, he may have had some reluctance. Unlike when he was leading Israel's army against the Philistines and in King Saul's good graces, he had very little to offer. Yet many people rallied to him. David was now an outlaw, and he had hundreds, maybe thousands of new mouths to feed and lives to protect. This new following would help him become king of Israel. How vital is followership, and what motivated so many to follow David into exile?

It must be said, that there is no leadership without followership. Behind every good leader are good followers, and in every good leader is a better follower. Joshua was a faithful follower of Moses, and Elisha was a committed follower of Elijah. It could be argued that both, Joshua and Elisha became better leaders because of how well they followed. Benjamin Franklin once said, "To learn how to lead, you must first learn how to follow." Aristotle put it strongly when he noted, "He who cannot be a good follower cannot be a good leader." What do we typically call a leader who won't follow or listen? A tyrant.

Contrary to the notions of some, a 'good' follower does not blindly follow a leader. That's slavery and subservience. They are not yes-men or yes-women who simply stroke a leader's ego and jump at every command. When Jesus compared his people to sheep, he was highlighting the closeness of the relationship, rather than blind followership.

Jesus' every intention was to equip and activate his first followers into leadership. As he said, "Follow me and I will make you fishers of men" (Matthew 4:19). He also said, "The works that I do shall you also do and greater works than these shall you do because I go to the Father" (John 14:12). To be a follower or a disciple of Jesus was about serving, learning, maturing, producing and leading. Jesus was replicating himself in his first group of followers, who in turn would do the same with another generation of followers. Being a good follower is vital for accomplishing a mission or a vision as well as acquiring personal growth and advancement. By following, we learn the value of what belongs to another as well as what it takes to lead. The first group of people that gathered to David helped to position him and themselves for a better future. What precipitated their following of David?

A stand-out characteristic of those who followed David was their willingness to leave so much behind. To say yes to David's leadership meant saying no to other essential things. They were willing to risk a lot to follow David. Good followers take risks. They are prepared to lay it all down for someone or something of great value. August Turak, in his article, *The 11 Leadership Secrets You Have Never Heard About*, noted that "Great followers seize the initiative." Of course, good leaders never take their followers for granted. The time and effort that people give to a leader, and their vision is precious indeed. Not only did David understand and cherish the sacrifices his followers were making, but he was also aware that each of them had their own difficulties.

It says that many of them were distressed, in debt and discontented. The Hebrew word for distress and discontent is *mar* or *marah*. The direct translation of this word is 'bitter,' but it also applies to those who have been in continued fighting, in mourning or crying. It conveys anguish of soul. Although it's important for any follower to be healthy enough to handle the responsibilities that come with serving, the fact that all followers have their own battles should never be overlooked. A servant-leader will also prioritize the needs of his followers. It's paramount that a leader knows his followers as individuals and not just as staff members performing a job description. Those who follow us are always more important than the goals we aspire to or the strategies we implement. This does not negate the priority of getting things done, it simply protects the relationship against 'getting undone.' It guards against followers becoming the proverbial 'means to an end.' I have seen this happen more times than I care to remember. There are few things more demoralizing to followers than the sudden awareness of being used and discarded by those they love and respect. How do we view those who we lead at home or at work? How motivated are they in the relationship? It's time to stop and answer that question for those who follow us.

Dan Pink, in his TED talk entitled, "The Puzzle of Motivation," noted how autonomy, mastery and purpose motivated productivity among followers. In other words, self-government, personal growth and the big-cause are primary movers for most followers. These three were very evident in the relationship between Jesus and his early disciples. Jesus continually relied upon their personal choices, relished their successes and refueled their horizons. This is what it looks like when we treat others as powerful and free. We respect their decisions, and we prioritize their growth. And this all happens in the atmosphere and environment of what author Simon Sinek calls the big "Why."

In his landmark book, *Start with Why*, Simon Sinek makes the argument for leaders who inspire. He said, "Those who truly lead are able to create a following of people who act not because they are swayed, but because they are inspired." According to Sinek, they are inspired by "Why." It's the bigger purpose, cause or belief that adds real meaning. What we do and how we do it can never inspire and empower people quite like, "why we do it." What is the big reason behind what you do? For my wife and me it's to turn heavenly reality into earthy actuality. It's about knowing God, loving people and demonstrating the goodness of Jesus anywhere. In over 37 years of ministry, we have seen thousands of followers inspired to become agents of change and leaders of industries. People have been energized more by the fuel of higher purpose than by any other single distinguishing aspect of our ministry. To let love lead, find out why.

14

You let love lead when conscience is more valuable than compliance.

Few leaders in the 20th century exemplified of conscience more than Dr. Martin Luther King. He led and fueled a movement that helped erase almost two hundred years of discrimination and segregation. In *A Testament of Hope: The Essential Writings and Speeches*, Dr. King is quoted as saying, "There comes a time when one must take a position that is neither safe, nor politic, nor popular, but he must take it because conscience tells him it is right." In other words, there is a point in every person's life when the inner voice of conscience must take a stand contrary to compliance. When we let love lead the conscience is not treated like some irrational child needing to be ignored. It is cherished and respected. James Madison, the 4th President of the United States, called conscience "the most sacred of all property." Paul told Timothy that the goal of his instruction was love from a pure heart, a good conscience and a sincere faith (1Timothy 1:5). This Greek word for *conscience* means: "to be conscious of right and wrong; to see completely." It's about knowing right from wrong and correctly applying that knowledge to our lives and relationships. History is loaded with leaders who fell on different sides of conscience – those who paid attention and those who didn't.

A conscience ignored is the seedbed of tyranny, while the conscience heeded is a birthplace of greatness. When the latter happens, we gain leaders like Florence Nightingale, William Wilberforce, Abraham Lincoln, Martin Luther King, Mother Teresa and Nelson Mandela, but when the former emerges society suffers under despots like Ivan the Terrible, Joseph Stalin, Mao Tse-tung, Adolph Hitler, Pol Pot and Saddam Hussain. What is true in one sphere of authority and leadership is true in all spheres. Whether home, church or business, respecting the conscience of others is paramount for building a culture of honor and promoting healthy relationships. Paul said to the Romans, "I am telling the truth in Christ, I am not lying, my conscience testifies with me in the Holy Spirit." Paul was asking the Romans to trust what he was saying because his conscience and the Holy Spirit were in agreement. He was providing no evidence other than what his conscience was saying. How refreshing it is to trust someone merely because they are a person of conscience. This sensitivity to God in our inner man has a sobering caveat. If it's not nurtured through obedience, it checks out. Like an advisor who is ignored, it quiets, then it quits.

Paul told Timothy that those who fall away from the faith

become seared in their conscience as with a branding iron (1 Timothy 4:2). It was well known that searing with a branding iron would leave the burned area without feeling. It was also common knowledge that the Romans branded slaves to identify them as their property. Paul is highlighting what happens when we ignore our conscience–when we say no to our God-given moral sensor. We not only lose our ability to feel the rightness and or wrongness of something, we also take on the mark of another identity. To choose contrary to our conscience is to act against divine design. There is nothing the enemy of our soul wars against more than our most authentic self. Making choices against our conscience will lead to thoughts, beliefs and behaviors that contradict who God created us to be.

Human history proves this over and over again. The nobility of humanity has often been hijacked by the nihilism of inhumanity. The early compromises of leaders in pre-Holocaust Germany is a case in point. Among other things, failure to speak out, pressure to conform and blind deference to authority contributed to the Jewish Holocaust. It did not happen overnight. It was a gradual process of ignoring conscience until people ignored life itself. This was false identity on steroids. Although most people have never participated in this level of identity carnage, many have lost their way by yielding to the pressures of strong personalities in corporate structures. There is nothing inherently wrong with a corporate identity. We all share an identity with others in specific communities. Who we are together is essential for success in life. The problem comes in when decisions, behaviors or actions in our corporate environments contradict other essential core beliefs or values. This has led to a deterioration of the soul known as 'burnout.'

According to Christina Maslach and Michael Leiter, authors of *The Truth About Burnout*, 'burnout' happens when there is a dislocation between what people value and what they do in the organizational environment. They went on to say that burnout represents the erosion in values, dignity, spirit, and will; an erosion of the human soul within a specific organizational context. Real health in the organizational environment is determined below the surface–in the conscience and core values of its leaders and employees. When love leads there is a congruence between what people fundamentally value and the systems and strategies of the organization. For example, if the core values of a company are 'quality service' and 'customer satisfaction,' then re-structuring just for profit's sake would never be a consideration. Incongruence and organizational dissonance would occur if executive salaries were suddenly more important than the quality of the product or the satisfaction of the customer. This conflict between values and actions is all too common in many organizations.

The leadership turnover in many churches and other faith-based organizations is indicative of this type of incongruence. An extensive study at the Francis A. Schaeffer Institute of Church Leadership Development found that seventy percent of leaders are so "stressed out and burned out that they regularly consider leaving the ministry." Research distilled from *Barna*, *Focus on the Family* and *Fuller Seminary* revealed that approximately fifteen hundred senior leaders leave the ministry each month because of moral problems, burnout and conflicts in their churches.

If fifteen hundred senior leaders are leaving their churches every month, how many more associate leaders and congregants are doing the same? The 'revolving door' for leaders and members becomes glaringly apparent when we consider that ninety percent of mega-church growth is generated by Christian's leaving other churches. Leaders at various levels in church organizations are leaving en masse, and burnout seems to be a significant contributing factor. We should never expect any leader to do what violates his or her conscience or is in direct contradiction to shared core values. In over 36 years of full-time vocational ministry, this has been the most common failure that I have witnessed among leaders in Christian organizations. For example, I was part of an organization which embraced strong relational values. In fact, being spiritual family was touted as one of the strengths of the organization. Unfortunately, when certain leaders sought to address problems in the organization, the operation of family became a bit more like *The Sopranos*. People were intimidated and/or shunned. Most of that dysfunction was the result of ignorance and immaturity rather than malice, and much has been learned and corrected over the years.

Honesty may not always be popular, but it beats a violated conscience. If the truth is told, courage happens when conscience is valued more than comfort. Time and time again, history has proven that one stirred conscience is more powerful than a million static opinions. The story of Dawson Doss, a conscientious objector in World War II, is a vivid picture of such power. He wanted to enlist as a medic to save lives and was persecuted by his fellow soldiers because he refused to pick up a rifle. His heroism was miraculous to say the least. He was the first conscientious objector to win a Congressional Medal of Honor. What he did in Gaum, on Hacksaw Ridge, is one of the greatest acts of courage in modern times. It happened because conscience was more important than compliance.

If we genuinely value individual conscience in our relationships, then we must resist the temptation to downplay, defend or deflect. Meaning, we should take the questions and concerns of others seriously. We must be quick to listen and understand what is being said rather than rifling off a diatribe of deflections. Even when someone's concerns about an issue are misinformed or misguided, taking time to hear them out is essential for maintaining trust and protecting the relationship.

15

You let love lead when others who are following you can discover, create and build even better than you.

It has been suggested that the best accomplishment of King David was not the giant he slew, the battles he won or the nation he governed, but instead, the warriors and builders who followed him. David's 'thirty mighty men' became heroes who did the impossible. Many of the men who served alongside David became greater in battle than him. According to the first Book of Chronicles, support from these men was an essential part of making him King (1 Chronicles 11:10). His son, Solomon, greatly exceeded him in wisdom and accomplishments. It says that Solomon's wisdom 'surpassed the wisdom of all the sons of the east and all the wisdom of Egypt" (1 Kings 4:30). Men came from every kingdom to hear his wisdom and see his work. The Queen of Sheba was so amazed by what she saw that it literally took her breath away. When love leads, an atmosphere conducive to the success of others is a hallmark characteristic. More specifically, discovering, creating and building become the domain of the generations that follow.

This highlights the role and necessity of multigenerational thinking. Few modeled this more than the Apostle Paul. Although not explicitly stated, the language used in the Book of Acts, I Corinthians and I&II Timothy implies that Timothy was converted through Paul's ministry during his first missionary journey. Paul recognizes the sincerity of Timothy's faith as first being evident in his grandmother, Lois, and then in his mother, Eunice. The fact the Paul frames Timothy's faith in generational language is noteworthy. In other words, Timothy's sincere faith, which Paul referred to as one of the goals of his instruction and mentoring, is seamlessly passed from one generation to the next.

According to Paul, these multigenerational relationships are where progress and succession can occur. He explicitly charged Timothy to take what he had seen and heard from him and pass it on to others–who would then pass it on to others (2 Timothy 2:2). Paul's knowledge of Jewish history influenced his exhortation. He knew how well Joshua had succeeded Moses, and that Joshua was not as successful in handing off to the next generation. It says that after Joshua there arose a generation that did not know the Lord or what he had done (Judges 2:10). Generational transfer was a hallmark of Hebrew culture. If the ceiling of one generation is meant to be the floor of the next generation then a proper exchange between young and old is paramount. Is it any wonder that God would introduce himself as the God of Abraham, Isaac and Jacob? In other words, he builds through and across the generations.

A New Testament version of the complementary nature of different generations is found in 1 John 2. John writes, "I am writing to you children...young men...and fathers." The faith of a child, the fight of a young man and the foresight, insight and hindsight of a father are included in the process of growth and productivity. Put differently, the courage of youth and the character of maturity are reciprocating and reinforcing qualities in multigenerational progress. Laboring with different generations in mind represents both the receiving and the giving sides of learning and leadership. Not only do leaders require mature and experienced input for success, they also need a successor to further the process of improvement. Progress is defined as advancing or moving forward in space, time, knowledge, character or matter. One generation benefiting from the successes and failures of a previous generation is essential to most productivity and progress.

The 'benefit exchange' between different age groups is not as one-sided as some tend to view it. There is little doubt that the strength and energy of youth require the wisdom and tempering of maturity to avoid becoming prodigal – but equally true, the tempered and wise elder requires robust engagement with the younger generation to prevent becoming rigid, sedentary and regressive. Moses and Joshua represent two generations that complemented each other for a higher purpose.

First, Joshua, the younger protégé of Moses was entrusted with leading a nation into the promised land. The commission given to Joshua was not just because of his youthful strength and unique skills, but also because of a rich investment from Moses. Second, the scripture makes a point of Moses' physical prowess. Although he was one hundred and twenty years old "his strength was not abated, nor was his eye dim." This was due, at least in part, to his continued service in mentoring the next generation. Studies on aging support the premise that the elder generation benefits enormously from physically and relationally demanding activities. The Harvard Study of Adult Development, the most comprehensive study on aging ever conducted, noted that regular exercise and close personal relationships with younger people are critical to healthy aging. Dr. George Vaillant, director of the Harvard study and senior physician at Brigham and Women's Hospital in Boston, noted that curiosity and creativity help transform older people into seemingly younger ones. When the older generation walks with the younger generation it reaps the benefits of physical and emotional rejuvenation. The younger generation gains knowledge, understanding and support while the older generation reaps joy and fulfillment. As Paul said to Timothy, "Longing to see you... that I may be filled with joy" (2 Timothy 1:4)

One of the purest examples of how this works comes from an old movie called 'Heidi.' Heidi was a young orphan girl who was sent to live with her grandfather after the death of her parents. She had never met her grandfather because he was a recluse living in the mountains. The first encounter between Heidi and her grandfather was little more than a 'vivacious bundle of curiosity meeting Stonehenge.' When Heidi first moves into the mountain cabin, her grandfather is entirely non-communicative and stoic. Yet a fantastic metamorphosis takes place. As he serves Heidi's basic needs (food and lodging), he comes to life emotionally. By the end of the movie, Heidi's grandfather is a new man, full of joy, purpose and passion. Specific life benefits can only be gained in reciprocating multigenerational relationships.

When the older and younger generations get separated from each other, we get 'Lord of the Flies' on the one hand and Grumpy Old Men on the other. In Lord of the Flies, we have young school boys who have been shipwrecked on a deserted island. Lacking any parental input they descend into barbarism. In Grumpy Old Men, two elderly friends, identifying with no one but themselves, regress into the worst kind of adolescent behavior. If there was any truth to the so-called 'generation gap' theory, some unbridgeable chasm between young and old, then we are all in serious trouble because God is called the "Ancient of Days."

God is not relatable and relevant to us because he is just like us, but because he possesses what we need. Different age groups are essential to one another because each generation has something the others lack. Wise and experienced military leaders lack the physical strength and fortitude of young soldiers to win battles. Parents and teachers need a child's curiosity and passion to pass on a legacy. God has designed features for specific age groups to act as provocateurs to other ages. The laughter of a child, the courage of a young man and the maturity of an elder are meant to leaven all of life. Going into the promised land of productive living requires a new level of generational partnerships.

When God called Moses to lead Israel out of Egypt, part of Pharaoh's opposition related to this multigenerational influence. In Exodus chapter 10 Pharaoh finally relented and said to Moses, "Go serve the Lord your God." He then asked, "Who are the ones that are going?" Moses told Pharaoh that they would be taking the young and the old with them. Although Pharaoh was prepared to release Moses and the young men, he was not about to let the children and the elderly go. Why? Because he knew that Moses could not leave Egypt without them. Once Pharaoh heard Moses' intention to take the children and the elderly, he accused Moses of having evil intent. In other words, he knew Israel intended leaving Egypt for good. When the generations are working well together, historical restraints get left behind for a better future.

PART III

WHO WE ARE TOGETHER

16

You let love lead when improvement is always the goal.

Throughout most of our lives, we are reminded that today and tomorrow should be better than the day before. Through proper eating, exercise and rest we are healthier; from learning, training and experience we usually acquire better jobs and opportunities; and by good communication, humility and sacrifice we have stronger marriages and families. Being productive or improving is not reserved for a select few. It operates almost anywhere we find people and resources. Improvement is a non-negotiable when love is leading.

Our first picture of the Godhead, in Genesis Chapters 1 and 2, demonstrates a partnership where things are being created–where improvement is one of the primary purposes. This should be the very nature of most relationships. In mathematics, one plus one equals two; in technology, software plus hardware plus electricity equals World Wide Web; in Athletics, strength plus speed plus stamina plus suppleness plus skill plus strategy equals Olympic champion; and in a family, its father plus mother equals Abraham Lincoln or Nelson Mandela. There are few things more motivating than progress, and nothing more basic to our relationship with God and others than our improvement.

When the apostle John wrote, "Beloved, I pray that in *all respects you may prosper* and be in good health just as your soul prospers" (3 John 1:2), he highlighted God's primary agenda for us: to advance or gain in everything. We are called to prosper in all things, and not just survive. Paul also underscored the priority of advancement when he wrote, "God causes all things to work together for good..." (Romans 8:28). The outcome of our working together should be 'good.' The word for good is *Agathos*. It means 'benefit' in the widest sense. Herein lie the standard and measurement for the partnerships we participate in. When our shared goal is improvement and gain, selfish posturing is significantly reduced. It provides protection against an individual's focus derailing the team's efforts.

Rather than making our specific roles or functions the primary focus, we hold ourselves and our skills accountable to acquiring growth and positive change. For example, in a team where the leader has strength in strategic thinking and execution, the need for relationship building cannot be ignored. What good is it if we meet our goal, and then lose the people and relationships that get us there? With few exceptions, it's a tragedy. Equally valid, the relationship savvy leader needs to keep his or her people skills accountable to the shared goals of the team. Catering to everyone's emotional whim is a recipe for disaster. It's the harmony of all three (strategy, execution and relationship building) that makes accomplishing goals possible. How many partnerships and teams have failed merely because individual personalities, positions or functions became more important than shared results? Way too many. How many spouses have made their thoughts, desires, personalities and capacities the sole fulcrum on which they leverage their marital future? The answer's the same, too many.

Of all the relationships created by God for the purpose of improvement, there is none as impacting as marriage and family. Marriage and family are the bedrock of society, and the way spouses engage one another will determine the strength of that rock. Sadly, many marriages are an exercise in one or both spouses attempting to replicate themselves in the other. Any subsequent crumbling is unavoidable. Although men and women are both guilty of setting their personal preferences and agendas as the marital centerpiece, men seem to do it with more regularity and blind arrogance. With few exceptions, most of the broken marriages I have witnessed had one thing in common, a husband who forgot that two people make one good marriage, not one person and their clone. Personal and shared improvement should be the measure for any marriage or family. I agree with Phyllis Koss who wrote, "Motto for the bride and groom: We are a work in progress with a lifetime contract."

This 'improvement quotient' in our relationships is often diminished when there is a lack of appropriate *value* and *vision*.

Meaning, if it's not important and inspiring it will get less attention and energy. Our level of value determines our degree of effort. There is a story about a dog that was known as the 'fastest dog' in the county. No other dog could come close to his speed. One day, the fastest dog in the county was chasing a rabbit. The rabbit managed to escape. After seeing the rabbit get away, all the other dogs began to laugh. In a mocking tone, they said, "You must be getting slow if you can't even catch a rabbit." The fastest dog in the county calmly retorted, "You need to remember, I was running for my dinner, but that rabbit was running for its life." The higher the value, the better the effort. Although we are naturally motivated by improvement and gain, there are life experiences and thought patterns that war against our better nature.

Most of us have experienced some form of rejection. The worst kind of rejection happens in families and other close relationships. The most common effect of this rejection is emotional pain and insecurity. The subsequent fear of failure or fear of rejection can prevent us from taking the steps of faith that are necessary to improve our lives. With that fear comes a lie that says "accomplishment is only for the other guy." It tries to convince us that harsh conditions around us are more powerful than how God has made us. It is true that circumstances can act as a significant impediment to growth, but it is not true that they are insurmountable. History is replete with examples of the seemingly unreachable being scaled. One of the great joys of life is how often people conquer the unconquerable. Like the story of Nick Vujicic. He was born without limbs. Physically, he is little more than a head and a torso, but in every other way, he is a giant.

After reading a newspaper article about a man overcoming a severe disability he began giving talks at his prayer group. Since then he has become an accomplished author, actor, movie producer and motivational speaker.

Another major impediment to our 'improvement quotient,' is when we lack vision. We were created with the ability to see something in our mind's eye before ever having it. Our imagination is more important than knowledge. As Albert Einstein said, "Knowledge is limited. Imagination encircles the world." He also said that "knowledge will get you from A-Z, but imagination will get you everywhere." This God-given ability to see bigger and better is either helped or hampered by the people we walk with. For example, immediately after Mary receives Gabriel's message about her giving birth to the Savior of the world, she goes to stay with her relative, Elizabeth. Elizabeth is a family member who had her own encounter with God. Their vision for the coming Messiah and his forerunner was nurtured in their relationship. They saw it together. On the other hand, Israel lost their ability to see the *promised land* due to listening to the evil report of the ten spies. By looking to those men, they could see nothing but giants and their own demise. The improvement we see or don't see will happen in the relationships we choose.

17

You let love lead when trust is more important than control.

I f I had to prioritize just one word for the next generation of leaders, which would I choose? Without a doubt, it would be 'trust.' Productivity is the primary purpose of a team, communication is its number one asset, but trust is its most valuable fuel. How many of us have ignored our fuel tank warning light to the point of running out of fuel? We are suddenly stranded in our brilliantly engineered automobile, which is about as helpful as an airplane without a pilot. When the fuel is gone that wonderful product of technology, our car, is pretty useless. Equally true, when the fuel tank of trust gets depleted, our ability to get things done is severely hampered. The great business consultant and author, Tom Peters, said that technique and technology are important, but adding trust is the issue of the decade. I would suggest that trust is the issue of the century. Author James O' Toole noted, "What creates trust, in the end, is the leader's manifest respect for their followers." We let love lead when having someone's trust is more important than gaining their compliance.

How many leaders understand the difference between compliance in a team and commitment to a team? The engine of a high-performance team is commitment, not compliance. Some leaders struggle to understand this. They can be oblivious to the fact that those around them are more compliant with their heads than committed with their hearts. It results in their employees or followers contributing well below their actual capacities. Some leaders don't make the connection between giving respect and gaining trust. They gauge the health of their team by how they're treated rather than how they treat others. They see their calling, vision and opinions as the epicenter of team performance, rather than what the team is called to accomplish together.

This can be a strange concept for some type-A leaders, whose verbosity can intimidate even the most capable of people. They demand respect, play the 'I'm the boss' card and patronize the heck out of any next-generation leader who attempts to think outside the box. In other words, their position, gifting and personality become the primary drivers for what gets done. Which means, shared values, mission and strategy get sacrificed at the altar of one fallible human being. Whatever happened to, "The Son of Man (Jesus) did not come to be served, but to serve and give his life as a ransom?" Was Paul using hyperbole when he wrote, "Do nothing from selfishness or empty conceit, but with humility of mind regard one another as more important than yourselves?"

There needs to be more honest reflection around the real nature of 'us.' Is our leadership, as Max De Pree so poignantly stated, "Abandoning ourselves to the strengths of others," or is it abandoning others to the 'tyranny of our strengths?' James O'Toole noted, "The ultimate in disrespect of individuals is to attempt to impose one's will on them without regard for what they want or need and without consulting them." When leaders behave domineering toward others the environment of 'us' becomes filled with insecurity, mistrust and self-preservation. That's not a team, that's a tragedy.

For any team that has productivity as its primary purpose, the solution is simple but challenging: a trust that fuels the practices of servant-leadership, mutual accountability and positive change. It's simple because we are all designed by God to give and receive trust; but challenging, because the trust inhibitors of fear and selfishness abound in many leader-follower relationships. Real trust cannot be taken; it can only be given and received. What are the qualities most suitable for trusting one another? Is it possible to guarantee a constant exchange of trust, no matter how contrary the circumstances are? The answer is, yes.

The chemistry of trust or the trustability of any relationship depends upon two variables: *character* and *competence*. Character addresses who we are and competence is what we are capable of doing. It takes both for appropriate levels of trust to emerge in a relationship. If I possess the acumen and skill to create a new business but have a reputation for not paying my debts, it's unlikely that any intelligent person would be willing to work with me. On the other hand, if I am known as honest and humble, but have absolutely no business experience, it's also unlikely I will find investors for my new business idea.

Stephen Covey, author of *The Speed of Trust*, describes character as the combination of integrity and intent. Meaning, we are a person of our word, and our motives and agendas are good and noble. For trust or confidence to characterize our partnerships, walking the talk and being motivated by the wellbeing of others and society are non-negotiable. Of course, it's our behavior that makes the loudest statement about our character. Is what you are doing modeling your good intent? Stephen made a good point when he said, "It is important to keep in mind that sometimes, unfortunately, poor behavior turns out to be the wrong execution of good intent." If we look too long through the lens of our good intentions, we are likely to tolerate for too long the effects of bad execution.

Paul Zak, who is the founding director of the Center for Neuroeconomic Studies and author of *Trust Factor: the Science of Creating High-Performance Companies,* conducted a long-term study to identify neurological signals that tell us when to trust someone. The study showed that higher levels of the brain chemical Oxytocin increased empathy and restrained the fear of trusting strangers. Through countless experiments and surveys, Paul and his team identified leadership behaviors that best engender trust in the organizational environment. Among them are recognizing excellence, give people discretion in how they do their work, intentionally build relationships, facilitate whole-person growth and show vulnerability.

There are few things more motivating than having one's efforts and accomplishments recognized and appreciated.

Zak's research showed that the most positive effect on trust occurs when someone excels and is celebrated for it. In *The Leadership Challenge*, authors James Kouzes and Barry Posner unpack the five practices of exemplary leadership. Included in these five practices is 'encouraging the heart.' Through decades of research, Kouzes and Posner identified encouragement as a non-negotiable part of successful leadership. For them, encouragement is the sincere recognition and celebration of someone's accomplishments. This can happen in many different ways, from simple verbal praise to material awards and celebratory rituals. Regardless of the manner we chose to show recognition; it should be sincere, consistent and measured. Pretentious praise or flattery will have the opposite effect on trust. It sends a message of superficiality or the hidden motives of self-interest. It's like getting water in your fuel tank. The vehicle will at best sputter along or at worst shut down completely.

Gordon McDonald said that being trusted is a greater compliment than being loved. Sometimes we assume people trust us just because they care about us. We should never confuse being loved with being trusted. My wife has never stopped loving me, but foolish decisions on my part have depleted our trust account on a few occasions. Whether with a spouse, a leader or a team, cultivating trust must be our number one priority. Trust energizes people and relationships. It will take us to higher levels of productivity as well as guard us against the hamstringing effects of pride and fear. When we let love lead we pursue trust over control.

18

You let love lead
when the power
of your values and
beliefs advise and
shape the form of
your organizational
structures, systems
and strategies.

'Who' we are together (power) and 'how' we are together (form) are equally significant. Connie and I are a married couple who love each other and share the same core beliefs and values. Our love, beliefs and values (power) have determined the lion's share of how we do our life together (form). Whenever Connie or I have taken actions contrary to our most basic relational values, conflict has resulted. The longer it took to rectify the incongruence the more damage our relationship incurred.

For example, when I decided to buy a house in Nashville

that was way beyond our means, it warred against Connie's conscience and our core convictions about financial responsibility. It became a source of mistrust and opened the door to several years of lurking tension in our relationship. The reason I chose the house was because it was very close to other families that we knew. We had just moved our family and ministry base from Johannesburg, South Africa to Nashville, Tennessee, and I planned to have a home as close as possible to other people in our ministry movement. I was so focused on that plan that I unwittingly ignored Connie's concerns and our financial capacities. Subsequently, we have rectified that area of conflict, and I have vowed to never again put our relationship in such jeopardy. To let love lead, the power of our values and beliefs must advise and shape the form of our relational styles, structures, systems and strategies.

The interactions between *'power* and *form'* are at the very heart of how most relationships either succeed or fail. First, we need a bit of clarity around this universal principle. There is no better place to begin than 'in the beginning.' "In the beginning God" (Genesis 1:1) is the ultimate power before form statement. All subsequent creation, with its countless structural and technological possibilities hidden in raw form, was made possible by the character and creative qualities of the eternal God. The unformed structures, tools and technologies, which God concealed in creation, were destined to materialize through the power of man's beliefs, values, character, abilities and efforts. The principle of 'power and form' is axiomatic. Meaning, *power creates form to serve the power*. After rain falls to the ground, the water gathers into one place, moving in a common direction. The pressure of that moving water (power) carves a channel (form), which continues to serve the water (power). Another example is Alexander Graham Bell's idea (power) to transmit speech electrically. That powerful idea stimulated research, experiments, knowledge and devices (form), which continue to serve more ideas (power).

All raw matter (form) had its beginning through the utterance of divine command (power). According to the writer of Hebrews, "The worlds were prepared by the word of God, so that what is seen was not made out of things which are visible (Hebrews 11:3)." In similar fashion, all subsequent 'forms' can credit their existence to *in the beginning man*. The primitive state of creation owes its current advanced form to a cadre of creative thinkers and doers who were looking for better ways to live out the power of their beliefs, values, ideas, visions, hopes and dreams. Our roads, buildings, bridges, houses, machines, products and technology were carved out of raw creation by humanity's sense of value, genius and effort. Since people are primarily motivated by what matters (values) to them, only things that matter (value) get a chance to inhabit useful matter (form).

What is true for marriages and families is equally true for most leadership teams and their organizations. All organizational structures, systems, strategies, products and tools owe their existence to powerful values, ideas, character and effort. Ever before the Apple computer and iPhone became world-class technologies they were the dream and relentless pursuit of leaders like Steve Jobs and Steve Wozniack. Microsoft, the world leader in computer and software technology, started in the mind and drive of childhood friends, Bill Gates and Paul Hansen. The Dream Center, open 24 hours a day, 365 days a year, reaching 50,000 people every week in Los Angeles by serving the spiritual and physical needs of the seemingly hopeless of society, was the dream of a young boy named Matthew Barnett. It is driven by the love and value that Matthew and his father, Tommy Barnett have for America's untouchables; the gang members, prostitutes, drug addicts, homeless, abused and impoverished. History is replete with how beliefs and values have shaped relationships, partnerships and organizations for the betterment of mankind. For Connie and I this has proven to be the case in over 37 years of church planting, organizational leadership and relationship building.

It started with Maranatha Ministries on university campuses in the United States. Because of our value and passion for reaching the next generation, we saw hundreds of college students having life-changing experiences. Even after 37 years, the strength of those values continues at the University of Arizona where we did our very first church plant. The church name has changed as well as the leadership team, but the power of those beliefs and values are still shaping the structures and strategies for reaching the students. As long as each subsequent generation of leaders imbibe the same core values and judge organizational change through the lens of those values, the work will continue to grow and prosper. This is proving to be even more accurate for the church we planted in Johannesburg, South Africa back in 1987.

From the Nation Building Conferences of the early 1990's to all the equipping strategies that followed, thousands of young people have been activated to live powerful and productive lives in their communities. The calling and commitment to reach the next generation of leaders in South Africa continue to progress through relevant and timely structural and strategic changes. This is being witnessed through outreach and development programs in all spheres of civil society. Although many changes have taken place with their systems and tools, their shared beliefs and values are providing the anchor and the drive towards greater fruitfulness. The impact of this power/form relationship continues to be evident in our newest church plant, Journey of Grace in Cape Town, South Africa.

About 5 years ago, Connie and I embarked on a new church plant with a handful of fabulous ladies and one elderly couple. Although each of us had many years of local church experience, and we knew what the structure of a local church should look like, we chose to prioritize values, people and experiences before venues, programs or events. Instead of renting a building for Sunday services, we met in a few different homes during the week. There is nothing wrong with buildings and programs, we all need them, but we wanted to lay the right foundation of value. Although Connie and I were leading the small gatherings, our time together was about everyone exercising their faith and demonstrating the goodness of Jesus in their daily lives. Whatever structure or strategy that followed would have to serve that passion and purpose.

The real test came when Connie and I needed to go back to the United States for 2-3 months. Would this small community of believers continue to gather and grow? To our great joy, it did. In spite of our absence, the people took responsibility for the values and the vision. When we finally booked a larger facility for Sunday services we had a culture that was rooted in personal responsibility, relationships and experiential faith. It made our Sunday gatherings supplemental to our life journey together, rather than the central focus. It helped us to create a structure that was a servant to the values and not the other way around. This relationship between power and form has become evident through so many aspects of our Journey of Grace culture. The most significant is how we apply biblical governance in the local church.

At Journey of Grace, our leadership and decision making is judiciously disseminated throughout the entire church. Our governance consists of Ephesians 4 ascension gift ministries (full-time vocational ministers), pastoral leaders (elders), administrative leaders (deacons), staff (secretaries, interns, etc.) and body ministry (equipped and empowered members). Decisions are made by those who have the responsibility for any area of service. We do not allow bottlenecks to be created around the 'hierarchy of a few' (senior pastors, elders, deacons, boards). Our shared purpose, values and vision guide the bulk of our decision making. Meaning, our leaders are trusted to adopt structures, strategies and tools that reflect and complement who we are. They do not need to run to the 'hierarchy of a few' for approval.

This governance model is driven by kingdom values rather individual callings, gifts and styles. We begin with our value for God's Presence rather than our preference for good programs. We see what God is doing, and we build structures to serve that, rather than create a structure and hope that God will fill it. We can often get ahead of the Holy Spirit just because that's what doing church has always looked like. How do you know if it's something God wants you to do? Sometimes you don't know for sure, but here are a few guidelines for discerning what God is breathing on. Besides simple obedience to the Word of God and your conscience, if you can answer 'yes' to the following questions you can be pretty sure the Holy Spirit is on it.

A. Is it what you are called and graced to do?
B. Is it edifying in your relationship with Jesus?
C. Is it edifying in your relationship with those you are building with?
D. Does it serve the needs that you are responsible for?
E. Can you find time and space for it in your current calendar and current activities?
F. Does it reflect your core beliefs and values?
H. Does it have the buy-in from others around you?
I. Is there faith for it and peace surrounding it?

This model is also rooted in the value of honor, which is the accurate recognition and receiving of the worth of another. Every person is unique and special, and has been created by God to hear his voice and bring His kingdom. Any structure or strategy we adopt has that reality in mind. For example, our Bible School focuses on people being activated supernaturally rather than just educated informationally. It makes everyone a functional partner rather than a loyal spectator. Because honor is the driving value, and not equality or egalitarianism, it enables us to build exclusive leadership elements based upon specific focuses, graces and abilities (worship, outreach, finance, preaching, pastoral, etc.). The value of honor helps us to draw the best out of everyone without acting like everything can be done by just anyone.

Prioritizing the value of honor makes sure the organization of the church isn't the sole measure for what the organism of the church (people) is doing. Meaning, what the Holy Spirit calls people to do, can and should happen beyond the structures of the local church. It's about the church, the people, in the trenches of their daily lives. The best evidence of success for this model isn't how much we can put on an organizational chart, but how much of Jesus people can experience in their families, workplaces and communities.

Because God's government is family, we value the person and relationship more than the position they occupy. This relational/family value means that who you are is infinitely more important than what you do. It means you can step out of a leadership position and not lose the relationship. It means you can mess up and not be rejected. It means you have the power to clean up your messes. We don't just see a skill and a job description, we see a family member.

Finally, this model prioritizes productivity over maintenance. We do not build around past successes, we build upon them. Maintenance is fine for keeping financial records or cleaning church facilities, but it's an enemy to advancing the kingdom and activating God's people. This creates a leadership structure where positive change can become a constant. Challenging our processes and enabling others is a big part of this values-driven leadership model. No one is there to just fulfill their calling or advance their agenda. The focus is doing better with what God has given to us as a team or a community. Having this values-driven culture will shift the nexus of control from a handful of full-time leaders to a Holy Spirit saturated full-time church.

To let love lead, our core values and beliefs need to remain front and center. This power-form framework has questions that need answering. What are the most essential values in the team or organization? Does everyone know what our values mean? What is the purpose, mission or vision for living out these values? What strategies are in place for living the values and accomplishing the mission? Are there any behaviors or actions taken by leaders or followers that are contradictory of the shared values? What are we doing to better model and celebrate our values? Answering these questions will help sustain an effective and progressive team culture. It will further our God-given purpose as well as guard against the trappings of groupthink, selfish ambition and institutionalism. It will let love lead.

19

You let love lead when relationships are never optional.

What came first, the chicken or the egg? The chicken of course. Science finally caught up with the Bible's account of creation. Scientists in Britain used a supercomputer called Hector to examine the finer details of an eggshell. They discovered that a protein, which is only found in chickens, was the catalyst for the shell's formation.

In the same way that a chicken is essential to the formation of an egg, relationships are indispensable to the health and well-being of people. As unique and special as each of us are, apart from relationships we do not exist. We are the product of heavenly and earthly relationships. The Godhead (Father, Son and Holy Spirit) made our existence possible, and our parents made us. Of course, there would be no relationships without the individual, but the value hidden in every person gets discovered, extracted and experienced within various kinds of relationships. Whether marriage, family, friendship or work, our willingness and ability to prioritize our connections is one of the most ubiquitous features of our human condition. A successful life is so much more than the brains we have – it's also about the brains we can borrow.

The African cultural ethic of Ubuntu reflects this relational priority. The word comes from a Xhosa proverb that means, "A person is a person through other persons." It emphasizes the relationship as the primary focus for growth and productivity. Meaning, the nature of who we are together is the progenitor of the new and improved. Rather than dismissing the importance of the individual, relationships are the vehicle for attaining the best versions of ourselves.

While using the metaphor of a physical body, the Apostle Paul told the believers in Ephesus that "every joint supplies according to the proper working of each individual part" (Ephesians 4:16). Although Paul was referring to how the whole body is fitted and held together (by our joints), it also means that our joints give us the flexibility and movement necessary for life and productivity. We could have the brain of a Nobel Prize winner, the cardiovascular system of an Ironman athlete or the strength of an Olympic weightlifter, yet without healthy joints, we will accomplish nothing and go nowhere.

Taking this body illustration one step further: being in a body relationally is very different from just hanging around organizationally. At various times your coat gets to hang out with your body. It enjoys the shape and movement of your body. It gets to go where your body goes. But if your coat gets a stain or a tear the life and power that's flowing through your body will not be able to remove the stain or repair the damage. Equally true, some things never get fixed or improved for us when we are not connected deeper than just 'hanging out.' Joints are deep tissue relationships between two or more parts. They consist of a diversity of parts, structures and fluids that depend upon their similarities as well as their differences. The structure of our bones provide support, while our tendons connect bone to muscle, our ligaments connect bone to bone, and our muscles provide contraction for movement. Equally essential are the blood vessels, nerves and lymph nodes. Without these shared components the knee would not function at all. They provide life, feeling and healing. Our blood brings life-giving energy and nutrients, our nerves keep up communications with the command center of the brain, and the lymph nodes filter out any unhealthy substances.

In like fashion, what we share together brings life, understanding, health, strength and productivity. There are few things more important for leaders to do than helping people find their fit. Not all relationships are right, but without the right relationships we can't live or lead well. The key here is to have a high value for relationships as well as to recognize which ones are essential.

Our value for most things is influenced by several criteria. When something is more costly, we ascribe more value to it. If something is rare and needed by many people, it becomes extremely valuable. Although most relationships aren't rare, they are costly and needed by everyone. They are expensive because they require time, humility, energy, courage and resources; and needed by everyone because no person is an island. Steve Moore and Tim Elmore put relationships or partnerships into a simple four-stage format: *friendship, formation, functioning* and *fruitfulness*. Although some partnerships do not require friendship, like managers and their workforce, when we let love lead a connection of hearts is non-negotiable. That doesn't necessarily mean you will do meals and vacations together, but it does mean seeing one another as valuable and special. It does mean prioritizing each other.

The *friendship stage* is more about chemistry. It's a real desire to be together and a willingness to prefer one another. I often refer to this stage as 'leaning into the grace.' When there is a 'good fit', it's usually easy to be together. There is a grace for drawing close. There is some degree of intimacy. The Latin root is *intimus*. It denotes openness and vulnerability. If we don't allow people into our story, we are unlikely to write new and better chapters. Mother Teresa said it best, "You can do what I cannot do. I can do what you cannot do. Together we can do what's never been done before." Friendships are the amino acids for building a preferable future.

The *formation stage* is more about the uniqueness of each person in the partnership. It's kind of like a rugby team going through various drills for different positions on the team. After an intense warmup together, the backs are running maneuvers, and the forwards are practicing their scrums, mauls and rucks. Both the backs and the forwards are thrilled that their team members in other positions are good at what they do. They deeply value the contribution they all make.

The strength of any relationship rises by answering this question in the affirmative: "Do I need you?" The bigger the yes, the better the effort, the bigger the win.

The *functioning stage* is about real cooperation. It's about shared purpose, mission and strategy. What we are doing together is front and center. Everyone and everything has a purpose. A rugby team exists to play rugby. They work together to move a ball effectively and efficiently towards the opposition's try line. They also work together to prevent their opponents from crossing their try line. The more they focus on their primary purpose, the better they do. All relationships need specific purpose and focus. Our purpose is the reason we exist or the reason we are together. It's more about who we are, and not just what we do. We play rugby because we are rugby players. It gives meaning to why we exist. Victor Frankl, in his book, *Man's Search for Meaning*, talks about his experience in a concentration camp during World War II. He noticed that the prisoners who were more likely to survive had specific goals or purpose. The best teams and most robust partnerships are anchored to a shared purpose for being together. The meaning for a rugby team is only found when playing rugby.

Of course, the rugby team has another stage that it aspires to; playing well enough to win. Moore and Elmore call this the *fruitfulness stage*. What would a ruby game be without goals? Pointless! Improvement and winning are as necessary to the relationship as are the players and the coaches. No one goes to a rugby game to just watch two teams running aimlessly on a field. They go to see their team win. They want to see their team play better than the week before. An essential relationship is one that includes opportunity and ability for improvement. If you are in a relationship where growth is stagnant and status quo is the primary metric, you may want to re-think the relationship. A couple that is not growing in marriage is a couple that's in trouble; leaders who are not developing or advancing in an organization are leaders who are being wasted, and teams that are not aspiring to new goals are usually not a team.

When we let love lead, relationships are primary. They are the vehicles for every good thing. The wrong relationships can have the opposite effect. Sometimes we are not good together. Some partnerships are dangerous and damaging, but at the end of the day 'who we are together' is the master key that unlocks a better tomorrow.

20

You let love lead when someone bigger and better than all of us makes it work.

W
e love because God first loved us. In the Song of Ascents, Solomon wrote, "Unless the Lord builds the house, they labour in vain who build it; unless the Lord guards the city, the watchmen keeps awake in vain (Psalms 127:1). The role of God the Father, Son and Holy Spirit in our leadership journey cannot be emphasized enough. We can adopt great values, apply right principles, employ good people and implement best practices and still fall flat. For love to lead, God, who is love, must be central to our journey.

One of the best illustrations of this point comes from the story of Jesus and the rich young ruler. The man runs up to Jesus and says, "Good teacher, what should I do to inherit eternal life?" (Mark 11:17). This encounter between Jesus and the young man has been used to illustrate the trappings of materialism. As appropriate as that may be, there is something much more revealing and powerful in the story. When we take a closer look at what he says and does, as well as Jesus' response to him, some beautiful qualities emerge. This young man is quite extraordinary.

His first approach to Jesus reflects passion, humility, respect, honesty and trust. He runs to Jesus and then kneels down before him. There is nothing in the language of the scripture that suggests pretentiousness. The young man is showing signs of urgency and submission. When he asks, "What shall I do..." he was genuinely looking for Jesus to teach him. He was honest about what he didn't know and totally open to what Jesus did know. The man's character is further evident through a literary tool that is used by the author, Mark. He uses a 'triple repeat' for emphasis. In verse 17 it reads, "...a man ran up to *Him* and knelt before *Him* and asked *Him*..." The word 'Him' is used three times in one short sentence. Although there is a group of people around Jesus, Mark is highlighting the man's focus and singlemindedness. Once again, we are seeing the man demonstrate noble qualities.

Then, after Jesus answers his question by highlighting six commandments that must be kept, he tells Jesus that he has kept them all from his youth up (Mark 10:19-20). In other words, verse 19 is an accurate picture of his character. Immediately after the man's response, Mark uses another tripe repeat, "Looking at *him*, Jesus felt love for *him* and said to *him*..." (vs. 21). Also, this word 'looking' is a unique word. It is equivalent to Isaiah 66:2 that reads, "But to this one will I look, he who is humble and contrite of heart." We are witnessing lots of godly character in this young man. From verse 19 we see that he has kingdom values and morals, he loves and respects family and he has good business practices. To top it off Jesus invites him to join his team of followers.

Of course, the story comes to a climax when Jesus says, "One thing you lack: go sell all you possess and give to the poor....and come, follow me" (vs. 21). The man became grieved and left. The usual assumption is that this was just about his material possessions; that he was unable to part with what he owned. But we know it wasn't just about money because of how the disciples responded. After Jesus said, "How hard it is for those who are wealthy to enter the kingdom of God," the disciples retorted, "Then who can be saved" (vs. 26). They had already left their material possessions to follow Jesus, so the wealth Jesus was referring to was not just material riches. The word Greek word for *wealth* is *Krema*, and it means "anything useful and beneficial." This can apply to the wealth of our internal property like character, talents, skills and experience. Jesus told him to sell his possessions to expose his faith in the wrong stuff. Meaning, you can't have kingdom life just because you have great character. This man had faith in good things, but the wrong good things.

The key here is when Jesus said, "*One thing* you lack..." (vs. 21). What did this man lack? He lacked Jesus. He had faith in everything but Jesus. He assumed that he could follow Jesus' quality of life because of his quality of character. It takes Jesus to follow Jesus. Responding to his disciple's question, "Then who can be saved," Jesus said, "With man this is impossible" (vs. 27). It's impossible to live like God, and that's why Jesus died for us. Christianity is not us living for Jesus, it is Jesus living through us. It's not faith in our character, or any other possession, it's faith in Christ alone. Paul was owned and operated by this fact. He told the believers in Philippi, "I have learned the secret of having abundance and suffering need. I can do all things through Him who strengthens me" (Philippians 4:12-13). He drove the point home when he said, "But by the grace of God I am what I am...; but I labored even more than all of them, yet not I, but the grace of God in me" (1Corinthians 15:10). If we are only leading from the strength of our character we are following ourselves more than following Christ.

We find this same quality in leaders like Moses and David. When God told Moses that he would not be among them when they traveled into the promised land, Moses strongly objected. He said, "If your presence does not go with us, do not lead us up from here" (Exodus 33:15). Moses refused to trust anything other than God being with them. Certainly, Moses and his delegated leaders had some degree of capacity for leading Israel into the promised land. God even guaranteed them angelic protection along the way. But it would not be enough. For Moses, it would be a disaster. He went on to say that they could only be distinguished from all the other people on the earth by God's presence being with them. For the task at hand, Moses refused to trust anything other than God.

Before David was selected to serve King Saul as a musician and an armor bearer, his résumé was presented to King Saul by one of the King's servants. It said that David was a skillful musician, a mighty man of valor, a warrior, one prudent in speech, had a handsome appearance and that the Lord was with him. Although being a musician was the most essential skill needed for the job, David relied on something much greater than natural talents and experience. For David, the Lord being with him was central to his success. When David fought Goliath, he made it very clear that it was the Lord who would deliver him. When we let love lead, God, who is love, is central to everything we do.

Jesus called a child to himself and said, "Truly I say to you, unless you are converted and become like little children, you shall not enter the kingdom of Heaven" (Matthew 18:3). The faith of a child is actually the most essential and powerful form of faith. Most children don't place confidence in personal skills, material possessions, accomplishments or fame – simply because they don't have any. The bulk of their faith is in the benevolence of others towards them, like parents, siblings or teachers. A story is told of a very successful man who was being interviewed by a reporter. The reporter asked, "What can you attribute all your success to?" The man responded, "Jesus loves me this I know." In a tone of disbelief, the reporter asked, "You mean to tell me that all of your success is because Jesus loves you?" "No," said the man, "Because this I know." When we let love lead, God the Father, Son and Holy Spirit are central in everything. Faith in Christ alone is what saves us and what undergirds us through all of life.

CONCLUSION

How can I conclude something as deep and impacting as 'let love lead?' The answer is, I can't. Leadership is as vast a subject as the earth itself, and love is as endless as our God and Savior who models it. But what I can do is shout from the rooftops that *let love lead* is a journey that never ends. It removes the shackles of fear and supplies your *expedition of hope and change*. When you say 'yes' to the better person that God has made you and others to be, you literally activate heaven on earth. Behind every set of eyes (yours included) are mountains to be scaled, oceans to be explored, works of art to be discovered and epic stories to be shared. To love God, yourself and others is the adventure of a lifetime.

In this book, you have read some of what it looks like when you *let love lead*. It offers a guide for those of us who are looking for a city, an organization or a team whose architect and builder is God. God can build anywhere, but He doesn't build just anything. This book gives some evidence to what it looks like when God, who is love, is building with us. As you apply these to your own life, more chapters will be added. How will you finish this statement?

"When I let love lead _____

_____.

John Maxwell says that "everything rises and falls on leadership." I contend that it always rises when love leads, and it always comes short when it doesn't. The Holy Spirit inspired Paul to write, "Love never fails" (1 Corinthians 13:8). This word 'fail' is more than just a setback, a serious mistake or a defeat. It literally means to "fall from grace" or to "fall into ruin." When love is our partner that can never happen. Wow, think about that! When we love, we cannot fail. We may not always have the outcome we were planning for, but failure cannot happen. We have been seated with Christ in heavenly places. And because we are seated so high, there is no place His love can't lead. This is what it means to live from heaven to earth. Whether in our families, professions or communities, letting God's love lead us is about as close to heaven as we will get before passing into glory at the end of our lives. Let Love Lead!

www.ingramcontent.com/pod-product-compliance
Lightning Source LLC
LaVergne TN
LVHW051412080426
835508LV00022B/3049